Sister Seonaid
        Professed 21st April 1994

'I thank my God for you,
every time I think of you'
                        Phil. 1.3

            Edward . Majorie

BORDER LANDS

David Adam was born in Alnwick, Northumberland, and is now Vicar of Holy Island. During a long period as Vicar of Danby in North Yorkshire he discovered a gift for composing prayers in the Celtic pattern, and since 1985 has published four very popular collections of prayers and meditations based on material he has used with many groups from his own parishes and on retreat.

This book
is a selection from
David Adam's
previous four books, also published by
Triangle/SPCK

The Edge of Glory: Prayers in the Celtic Tradition 1985

The Cry of the Deer: Meditations on the Hymn of St Patrick
1987

Tides and Seasons: Modern Prayers in the Celtic Tradition
1989

*The Eye of the Eagle: Meditations on the Hymn 'Be thou my
Vision'* 1990

The Best of
DAVID ADAM

Border Lands

Illustrated by
Jean Freer, Peter Dingle
and others

Anth [P/W." 12]

808.8

First published 1991
SPCK
Holy Trinity Church
Marylebone Road
London NW1 4DU

Copyright © David Adam 1991

British Library Cataloguing in Publication Data
Adam, David
Border Lands: the best of David Adam.
I. Title.
242

ISBN 0-281-04541-0

Typeset by Rowland Phototypesetting Ltd
Bury St Edmunds, Suffolk
Printed and bound in Great Britain by
BPCC Hazell Books
Aylesbury, Bucks, England
Member of BPCC Ltd.

Contents

————

Introduction   vii

BEGINNING – BETWEEN EBB AND FLOW   1

BETWEEN DARKNESS AND LIGHT   13

BETWEEN SEARCHING AND KNOWING   61

BETWEEN WEAKNESS AND STRENGTH   115

BETWEEN DYING AND LIVING   167

Notes   239

To Connie and Jackie,
Border Land workers

Introduction

For much of my life, I have lived on what is called 'marginal lands'. These are areas where some are afraid to go forward and some refuse to venture, areas where many think they have reached their limits, but where others see and reach beyond. I have been used to far-reaching views where you feel that it is only your own short sightedness that prevents you seeing deeper or further. It is exciting to walk the very edge of things, whether it is a cliff top or an idea. There is something invigorating about treading on the edge of the familiar, pressing beyond the border of the known, and reaching out to new horizons. If we do not adventure, there is something in us that will remain unsatisfied, and perhaps die. I like places where the elements meet, where the wave crashes or laps on the shore, where the earth touches the sky, where day turns into night or night into day. At such meeting places there is always an interaction and an encounter for those with eyes to see. Such places are always exciting, if we allow them to act upon us.

In our world we seek to protect ourselves from the extremes – or weather or of experience. We are told to keep away from the edge, for it is dangerous. So we lose out on adventure. I was lucky at College to read Alec Vidler's book *Christian Belief* where he said of the Holy Spirit:

> It is the work of the Holy Spirit to disturb a man or an institution that is becoming settled or stiff; to break up what was taken for a fixed philosophy of life or a satisfactory routine of habit, in order that he may build up something further and better. The Holy Spirit works like an acid on all complacency. He

points and presses men onwards into the unknown. 'It is good once in a while' said Kierkegaard 'to feel oneself in the hands of God, and not always and eternally slinking around the familiar nooks and corners of a town, where one always knows a way out.

Today, we are very much in danger of producing 'midlander' mentality and emotions: those of safe people who have never been all at sea or experienced the 'cliffs of fall' (as the poet Gerard Hopkins described the mind's mountains of grief). We avoid being frontiersmen and women in case we are shot at, though more often than not we are shot at by our own side if we dare to cross boundaries. Yet in reality, life is for ever taking us to the edge of things. Borders may be hard to see or define, but we forever cross into new lands. Frontiers are still exciting places and everyone should be encouraged to explore them: the border lands are there for us all to enjoy.

It is interesting to see how often Jesus is in the border lands, between countries, between heaven and earth. He is found on the fringes of society, with lepers, with publicans and sinners. He is himself the 'scorned and rejected of men': edged out of the synagogue and Temple, edged out of the city, edged out of life to be 'outside the city walls'. He crossed the border between life and death, and returned. Jesus appears to a group whose 'nerves were on edge'. He appears at the end of the day and the end of the journey. He appears by the seashore. He appears on the mountain top. So, ends become new beginnings; horizons challenge the limits of vision. When Jesus met the mad man of Gadara, he and his disciples had crossed many borders: it was the edge of another country, beyond a storm, beyond the graves, to the land of unreason and violence. Not only did Jesus enter this area, but there his powers were and are revealed. Jesus is still to be discovered on all the fringe areas of society. It is for this reason I find the border lands an exciting place to be.

It is my fascination with border lands which has produced such titles for my books as *The Edge of Glory* and *Tides and Seasons*, while *The Cry of the Deer* is about the call that comes from deep within us or from the great beyond calling us out. There is something in each that calls us to have the Exodus experience, to move out of safety and captivity into the unknown. We cross borders until we come to the promised land. Often the land we are looking for has always been our homeland, though we have not seen it or explored its borders. This is expressed by T. S. Eliot in *Little Gidding*:

> We shall not cease from exploration
> And the end of all our exploring
> Will be to arrive where we started
> And know the place for the first time.

In the *Eye of the Eagle* there is a desire to show that we can begin to 'see' the beyond that is in our midst. There are ways of increasing our sensitivity to the situation we are in. The more we become attuned to the other, the better chance we have of understanding the 'great other' who is God. The edge of glory is something that is always there, waiting to be discovered, calling to us in our dreams and yearnings. We need to learn again that is a great adventure to walk the edge of glory. All four books are about beginnings and endings, about shores, edges, turning points and horizons. Tides and seasons are what come to us all and affect us throughout each day. The tides of life and the world influence us, even if we fail to notice it. We are far more a part of the changes and chances of the world that most of us have recognised.

I believe that we are all called to extend our vision, our awareness, our sensitivities. Quite often we fail to 'see' because we have been unwilling to go far enough or deep enough. Quite often the statement, 'I do not believe' seems to mean, 'I am unable or unwilling to go any further'. It is amazing that so many of us think faith comes through 'natural growth' without work on our part. There is as much chance of having a strong and healthy faith without working at it, as there is to have a garden full of flowers if we leave it to nature. In the human life, as in the garden, weeds will dominate if we do not do some work. That is why every so often, in my books, I have produced exercises with which people can work at themselves to increase their awareness and vision.

For those who are willing to make the journey to the edges, the world and anything in it can still be the primary scripture, that which speaks to us of God. Before any books were written, God spoke through his creation, he revealed himself through the things of the earth. The signs were there for those who learn to read them. These signs are there still. But as with the written Scriptures, we have to learn to read and meditate on what is before us. So many of us today are illiterate when it comes to reading our own environment. If only our eyes are opened to see and read there is a fantastic depth to our lives and to every created thing; all things shine with the numinous. Even the common soil will still open blind eyes if we come in faith. If we cannot, or are unwilling to look out from our immediate little world to the beyond, then it will be very hard for us even to grasp a glimpse of the great beyond which speaks of God. If we are unable to begin to comprehend ourselves, how can we hope to understand the being of God? One of the sad comments on our times is we teach children to read books but often leave them unable to read themselves or the world around them. We often cover a great ground but rarely go very deeply. We need to heed the words of Eckhart when he said, 'We must learn to penetrate things and find God there'. The same Eckhart said 'Every creature is a word of God and a book about God'. I see it as much of my task, and my joy, to extend horizons, to endeavour to probe deeper, to see further, to be more sensitive to all that is around us. As a treader of the border lands, I know that glory is never far away and often I am on the very edge of it. I want to share this experience with others.

Quite often the 'other world' is only a step away waiting to be discovered. We can suddenly find we are in it, like Lucy in *The Lion, the Witch and the Wardrobe*, though we have to discover a means of entry to it. Lucy entered the 'otherworld' through the wardrobe; we may think that odd, yet Moses entered it through a burning bush, Isaiah through an empty throne. We have to find the place that allows us to 'see' beyond. Sometimes we can then return to that place time and time again for renewal, while on other occasions we will suddenly find that the place of the past no longer opens doors for us; we cannot live off past glories. In *The Lion, the Witch and the Wardrobe* the children are told:

> I don't think it will be any good trying to go back through the wardrobe door . . . you won't get into Narnia again by that route . . . don't go trying the same route twice. Indeed don't try to get there at all. It will happen when you are not looking for it . . . and don't mention it to anyone else, unless you find that they've had adventures of the same sort themselves.

We cannot manipulate the experience, but we can wait at the edge, we can remain sensitive and alert. All the time, the otherworld is there, in fact it is here, for he is here, and waiting for us. It does us good to ponder long this reality and not to get caught up in the fantasy of a God who is far off. We are on the very border lands of his kingdom, and he is bidding us welcome.

The Celtic church grew on the very borders of civilis-ation. Columbanus described his people, the Irish, as *ultimi habitatores mundi*, inhabitants of the world's edge. Their homelands were at fringes of the ancient world, yet they looked westward for the mystic island that might appear. Like St Brendan, some ventured into the great unknown, and possibly reached America. They became pilgrims 'for the love of God', reaching out and exploring new areas of his creation. Sometimes aggression from invaders forced the Celtic nations into marginal land, on other occasions little bands of monks chose such places. Even when they were offered a way-out place to build a monastery, some had to go a stage further and create a 'disert'. The disert place of retreat was set up to discover the edge of glory, to experience the beyond that is in our midst. 'Diserts' are set up not to run away from what is going on, but to experience in greater depth the reality that is about them. We are bombarded today by so much fantasy that it is necessary again to take time to be aware of the realities that are about us. Somehow the Celtic peoples, due to their history, have been able to keep an awareness of the 'other' far more easily than most other peoples. It was expressed in a beautifully simple way by a woman from Kerry in the south west of Ireland. When she was asked where heaven was, she replied, 'About a foot and a half above a person'. Such an awareness has us always treading exciting border lands.

We need heed the words of Jesus in St Mark's Gospel, 'The Kingdom of Heaven is at hand, repent . . .' (Mark 1. 15). The Kingdom is at hand and some are entering into it. The Kingdom beckons to us in the border lands of life and in the fullness of life. We are called to 'repent', to turn around, to have a change of mind and heart, that we may see what is in our midst.

If these thoughts and prayers are used to extend your horizon and reach into the border lands to the beyond in our midst, they will have served their purpose.

David Adam
Holy Island, Easter 1991

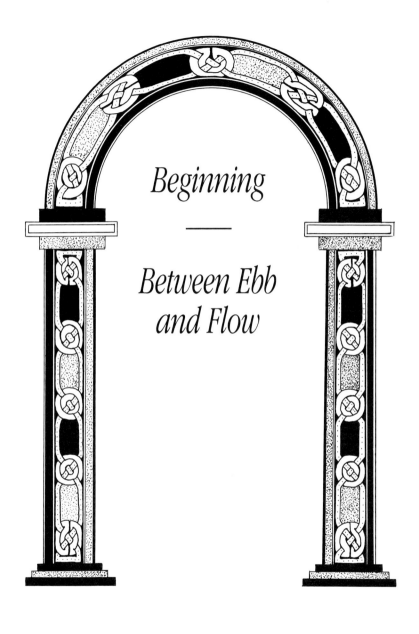

Beginning

——

*Between Ebb
and Flow*

Morning Light

God of the dawning,
Christ of the sea,
Spirit, giver of breath to me,
Trinity blessed, all praise to thee,
Giving this day of newness to me.

Bless me today body and soul,
Bless me today and keep me whole,
Bless me today in all that I do,
Bless my powers, they come from you.

Before Prayer

I weave a silence on to my lips
I weave a silence into my mind
I weave a silence within my heart
I close my ears to distractions
I close my eyes to attractions
I close my heart to temptations

Calm me O Lord as you stilled the storm
Still me O Lord, keep me from harm
Let all the tumult within me cease
Enfold me Lord in your peace

Opening Prayer

God be with us
Amen
The Lord be with you
And with your spirit too

The Father be with us
Amen
The Creator be with you
And with your spirit too

Jesus be with us
Amen
The Saviour be with you
And with your spirit too

The Spirit be with us
Amen
The Strengthener be with you
And with your spirit too

The Trinity be with us
Amen
The Sacred Three be over you
And with your spirit too

God be with us
Amen

Veni Creator

Come Lord
Come down
Come in
Come among us
Come as the wind
To move us
Come as the light
To prove us
Come as the night
To rest us
Come as the storm
To test us
Come as the sun
To warm us
Come as the stillness
To calm us
Come Lord
Come down
Come in
Come among us.

Tides and Seasons

Everything in this life is visited by its tides and seasons. This world is in a state of constant flux; all is flowing, changing. The more alive and alert the creature is, the more likely it is to be changing regularly. All of us are caught up in the pull of the ebb and flow of the whole of creation. In each of us there are many strong currents at work. We are a very small and frail craft in a mighty ocean. Yet we may be privileged to discover, in the ebb and flow, that nothing is lost, only changed. As the tide ebbs on one shore it flows on another. In the ebbing, the sea is not diminished: as one area decreases, another is increasing. The end of one thing always heralds the beginning of something new. In the same way the beginning of something marks the end of an old order.

Within this pattern, we need to see that we are not just a single sequence of tides: we do not begin with the one flowing and end on the ebb. We are more than an ocean with its ebbing and flowing: we contain within ourselves many ebbings and many flowings, many different seas and currents. We are a whole world of tides with many oceans, and at different levels at the same time. In times of diminishment especially, we need to be made aware of other shores, even of eternal reaches. For all of us, as long as we are alive there are always new horizons. In the tenth-century Celtic poem, 'The Old Woman of Beare', we see such a tide struggle at work:

> The flood wave
> And the second ebb-tide
> They have reached me.
> I know them well.
> O happy the isle of the great sea
> Which the flood reaches after the ebb!

But ageing and the feeling of guilt or rejection, makes her concentrate on the ebb tide. There is a tendency for all of us to let the world and experience diminish us. The Old Woman of Beare goes on:

> As for me I do not expect
> Flood after ebb to come to me.
> There is scarce a little place today
> That I can recognise:
> What was on flood is all on ebb.

This experience is echoed by most of us more than once in our lives – if not every day! There is a danger at the low ebb to feel we are all alone. Samuel Taylor Coleridge expressed it in his 'Ancient Mariner':

> . . . this soul hath been
> Alone on a wide, wide sea:
> So lonely 'twas, that God himself
> Scarce seemed there to be.

But the Christian does not stop there, even when God seems not to be. We are called to be aware of other tides, other shores. In this world, we are to say like John the Baptist, 'He must increase, I must decrease.' But that is limited to this world and its oceans. We believe in Jesus risen, and the eternal shore

> Where no storms come,
> Where the green swell is in the haven dumb . . .[1]

Or as expressed by a lesser poet, Arthur Clough:

> For while the tired waves, vainly breaking,
> Seemed here no painful inch to gain,
> Far back, through creeks and inlets making
> Comes silent, flooding in, the main.[2]

In this book[3] I have attempted to look at the different tides of life, believing that for most of the time all of the tides are at work in us.

I have chosen the approach of the Celtic Church

because I believe it has a great deal to teach us about the unity of the world and the Divine Presence in it. We are all still close to nature, though many of us are unaware of it, just as many are unaware of its Creator. But both are ever with us. The Celts sought to build an outer world which reflected their belief in the Presence and Oneness of God; a belief well summarised in the words of St Patrick to the princesses of Tara:

Our God is the God of all men,
the God of heaven and earth,
the God of sea, of river, of sun and moon and stars,
of the lofty mountains and the lowly valleys.
The God above heaven,
The God under heaven,
The God in heaven.
He has His dwelling round heaven,
and earth and sea, and all that is in them,
He inspires all,
He quickens all,
He dominates all,
He sustains all.
He lights the light of the sun:
He furnishes the light of light . . .

The Celtic Church saw and reflected a glory which we seem to have lost from the earth. Because of this belief they saw all things inter-related and interdependent. I believe we need to recapture that awareness, for man is not only out of tune with God, he is out of tune with the world and with himself.

In his book *The Tree of Life*, H. J. Massingham wrote:

If the British Church had survived, it is possible that the fissure between Christianity and nature, widening through the centuries, would not have cracked the unity of western man's attitude to the Universe.[4]

We need, once again, to rediscover the precious links between all living things; that there is a unity at the very heart of our world, and it can be experienced by each of us. Basic to that unity is a combination of God-awareness and what the world now calls ecology.

There is no doubt that we are caught up in cosmic, if not universal tides and seasons. We cannot control them all, nor can we stand apart, but we can seek to be more receptive and aware. We can affirm that we are influencing the whole of our world, as it is influencing us. We can also affirm that God is deeply concerned, for He loves His world. In looking at every tide it might make us face reality a little better. In this world some things do finish, and diminish; but

. . . For all this, nature is never spent;
There lives the dearest freshness deep down things;
And though the last lights off the black West went
Oh, morning, at the brown brink eastward springs –
Because the Holy Ghost over the bent
World broods with warm breast and with ah! bright
wings.[5]

Lord,

There are times when I need to be an island,
Set in an infinite sea
Cut off from all that comes to me
But surrounded still by thee.
Times of quiet and peace
When traffic and turmoil cease
When I can be still and worship thee
Lord of the land and sea.
Full tide and ebb tide
Let life rhythms flow
Ebb tide, full tide
How life's beat must go.

Lord,

I must be part of the mainland,
A causeway between me and others.
There are times when I can only find thee
In working with my brothers.
Times of business and industry
Freeing ourselves from captivity.
It's when we give a helping hand
We meet you, Lord of sea and land.
Ebb tide, full tide
Let life rhythms flow
Full tide, ebb tide
How life's beat must go.

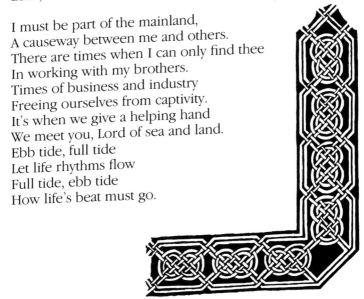

The Kingdom

Today, Lord,
     Thy kingdom has come.
In the quiet of the dawning
In the darkness we are scorning
In the newness of the morning
     Thy kingdom has come.

In my waking and my dressing
In my former sins confessing
In my life and its progressing
     Thy kingdom has come.

In this moment for the taking
In this day that we are making
In the evil we are forsaking
     Thy kingdom has come.

In meeting one another
In loving sister and brother
In seeing you Lord in the other
     Thy Kingdom has come.

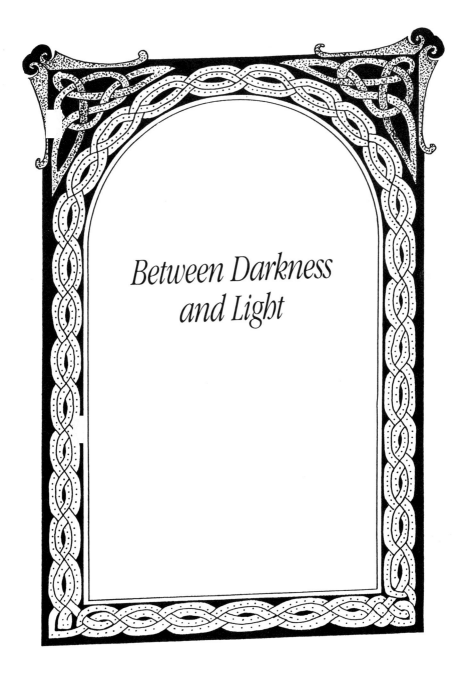

*Between Darkness
and Light*

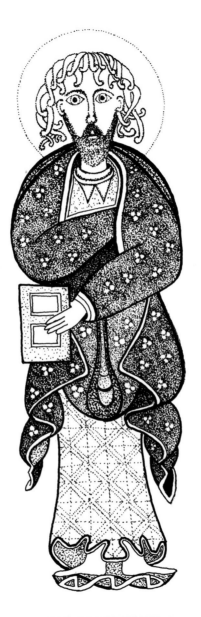

ST MATTHEW

Maker of All

You are the Maker
Of earth and sky,
You are the Maker
Of heaven on high.
You are the Maker
Of oceans deep,
You are the Maker
Of mountains steep.
You are the Maker
Of sun and rain,
You are the Maker
Of hill and plain.
You are the Maker
Of such as me.
Keep me, O Lord,
Eternally.

Teach me to see you, Lord,
In all things seen and heard,
In beauty of the heather moors,
In the singing of a bird.

Awaken me, Lord

Awaken me, Lord,
To your light,
Open my eyes
To your presence.

Awaken me, Lord,
To your love,
Open my heart
To your indwelling.

Awaken me, Lord,
To your life,
Open my mind
To your abiding.

Awaken me, Lord,
To your purpose,
Open my will
To your guiding.

Christ Everlasting Friend

Christ in my beginning
Christ there at my end
Christ be in my journey
Christ everlasting friend
Christ be in my waking
Christ at my repose
Christ in every action
Christ when eyelids close

Incoming Tide

We all experience the incoming tide. We left a world of darkness behind when we arrived on the shore of this world. Our birth was an incoming. Throughout our lives we will again and again be offered new experiences, new chances for change, and renewal. For all of us there will be new people to encounter and new places to visit. At all times there will be the coming of the great Other to us; God is ever coming into our lives. So we need to be aware of the coming and to rejoice in it. We should make sure that our life has a good inflow and is not 'all on ebb'. It is interesting to know that the Aid Woman on the Hebridean islands liked the child to be born if possible on an incoming tide. As soon as possible the child would be dipped in the incoming tide, expressing the simple desire that his or her life would freely flow.

The incoming tide marks the beginning of things, the springtime of our lives. It is necessary to keep a freshness and an openness at all times. The world will flood us with newness each day, we will be offered change and the challenge of change. Most people say they rejoice in the incoming tide, that it is far more acceptable than the outgoing. But, in fact, we all seek to control this tide as much as we seek to control the others. We filter out experiences and avoid certain encounters. There are many worlds about us but we seek to choose one. We allow clouds to gather around us that restrict our vision. This is as true of our material awareness as it is of our vision of God. It is as T. S. Eliot says:

Human kind cannot bear very much reality.[1]

There is a danger that Christians give the impression that they do not love the world, that we should flee from

18

the world. We need to proclaim strongly that it is God's world, that it is basically good, and that God himself loves it. The true monk of the desert never fled the world, only the game of trivial pursuits that so many persist in playing. It is easier to hide from the world in busy streets and air-conditioned offices than it is in the desert. It is harder to hide from the incoming tide when all surrounding cover has been removed. The true monk of the desert sought to enter deeper and deeper into life. This is to be the task of all of us. In *Hymn of the Universe*, Teilhard de Chardin says:

> Purity does not come in separation from but in a deeper penetration into the Universe . . . Bathe yourself in the ocean of matter; plunge into it where it is deepest and most violent; struggle in its currents and drink its waters. For it cradled you long ago in your preconscious existence: and it is the ocean that will raise you up to God.[2]

Let us learn not only to become more aware of what comes to us but to rejoice in it. To know each day that He comes and He seeks to make all things new.

I Have Seen the Lord

Where the mist rises from the sea,
Where the waves creep upon the shore,
Where the wrack lifts upon the strand,
    I have seen the Lord.

Where the sun awakens the day,
Where the road winds on its way,
Where the fields are sweet with hay,
    I have seen the Lord.

Where the stars shine in the sky,
Where the streets so peaceful lie,
Where the darkness is so nigh,
    I have seen the Lord.

The Lord is here,
The Lord is there,
The Lord is everywhere.
The Lord is high,
The Lord is low,
The Lord is on the path I go.

For a New Day

God of Time
God of Space
Fill this moment
With your grace.
God of Motion
God of Peace
From each sin
Give release.
God of Quiet
God of Might
Keep us ever
In your sight.

Dressing Prayer

This day I bind around me
The power of the Sacred Three:
The hand to hold,
The heart to love,
The eye to see,
The Presence of the Trinity.

I wrap around my mortal frame
The power of the Creator's name:
The Father's might, His holy arm,
To shield this day and keep from harm.

I cover myself from above
With the great Redeemer's love.
The Son's bright light to shine on me,
To protect this day, to eternity.

I pull around me with morning light
The knowledge of the Spirit's sight.
The Strengthener's eye to keep guard,
Covering my path when it is hard.

This day I bind around me
The power of the Sacred Three.

Morning Prayer

Lord you are in this place,
> Fill us with your power,
> Cover us with your peace,
> Show us your presence.

Lord help us to know,
> We are in your hands,
> We are under your protection,
> We are covered by your love.

Lord we ask you today,
> To deliver us from evil,
> To guide us in our travels,
> To defend us from all harm.

Lord give us now,
> Eyes to see the invisible,
> Ears to hear your call,
> Hands to do your work,
> And hearts to respond to your love.

Be thou my vision, O Lord of my heart.

———

I once worked in a coal mine deep in the Northumbrian earth. It had a strange atmosphere all of its own. But the most awe-inspiring thing was the darkness. It was so black when you turned your lamp off that you could not see your hand in front of your face. For a while in the area I worked there was no light at all except from the lamp fastened to my helmet. One day, while working on my own, I knocked the lamp hard against a stone and it went out. I was in total darkness with moving machinery near by. I hardly dared to move, only slightly backwards to the rough-hewn wall. It would have been easy to panic – or just to scream out – but I knew that very soon some fellow-workers would arrive. They would have lights and they would ensure that I was not left in the dark. I waited for what seemed an age – it was probably hardly five minutes. Then a light appeared. At first it was small and far away, like a pin-prick in the dark. But I knew it was coming in my direction. In fact, I could see three lights coming towards me. Soon my companions were attending to me, and in fact got the second bulb on my lamp working again.

It was not long after this, at New Year, that I heard for the first time:

> I said to the man who stood at the gate of the year: 'Give me a light that I may tread safely into the unknown.' And he replied: 'Go out into the darkness and put your hand into the hand of God. That shall be to you better than light and safer than a known way.'[3]

About then another quest began. I wanted to discover

a light that would shine in the darkness of the world – something or someone that would give me a better vision, in a world where the light seemed to be growing dim.

It was a bit later that I became fascinated with a story from the Old Testament. It is a story of the church having grown old; visions were rare, the old priest was almost blind. The children of the 'vicarage' had rebelled, as often seems the case. It seemed that the poor old church had little to offer. If anything, it needed looking after. Fortunately a woman saw that it was a place to bring her son and leave him there. The boy looked after the old man. At night he had to keep alert, to keep all his senses tuned for a call or a cry. In listening for the other person, the Great Other broke into his life. Perhaps he would never have known this fact if it were not for the old man, the custodian of the knowledge. Eli may have almost lost his sight, but he realised it was the Lord calling the boy. The nearly blind old man stood at the dawn of a new day, and though the lamp burned low, Eli handed on the light. He taught the boy Samuel to say, 'Speak, Lord, for your servant is listening'.[4]

I was to learn that those who listen carefully to others are in the best position for hearing the Great Other. A group of people in a similar state of awareness were the shepherds on the Bethlehem hills. They had all their senses tuned to the night and its movements. They were open and receptive. While they were keeping watch, the message came. But there was still a greater learning to come, that the light had never been far away. The Presence is always there. God is in His world and seeking to break into our unawareness, to shatter our blindness. In reality, neither we nor His world have lost His Presence or His glory. But we have lost our ability to see. We are like the man born blind and need pray, 'Lord, that I may receive my sight'.

There is a haunting song from the island of Harris in the Outer Hebrides. It was sung by a woman, a leper, who was an outcast from society, banished from her upland home to live on the seashore. Left alone on the fringes of the island, she discovered that she was not alone. Nothing could separate her from the immanent God, in whom she lived and moved and had her being. The transcendent had come down, God was incarnate in His creation, the Christ had come to Harris. In some strange way she knew this and was uplifted.

> It were easy for Jesu
> To renew the withered tree
> As to wither the new
> Were it His will so to do.
> > Jesu! Jesu! Jesu!
> > Jesu! Meet it were to praise Him.
>
> There is no plant in the ground
> But is full of His virtue,
> There is no form in the strand
> But full of His blessing . . .
>
> There is no life in the sea,
> There is no creature in the river,
> There is naught in the firmament,
> But proclaims His goodness . . .
>
> There is no bird on the wing,
> There is no star in the sky,
> There is nothing beneath the sun,
> But proclaims His goodness.[5]

She discovered, personally, that the Presence was 'not by conversion of the Godhead into flesh: but by taking the Manhood (and Womanhood) into God'.[6] In her own self she discovered 'the Word made flesh and dwelling among us', and she 'beheld His glory'. The light shone in her dark days. Her eyes had been opened and she shared the vision of the eye of the eagle.

Perhaps it is because we do not look often enough at the borderlands where worlds meet that we fail to discover what is beyond. We seem afraid of the shadows and the dark. We are unwilling to move out from our safe place. We do not like our securities or our ideas to be challenged. We are as afraid of a God that we cannot tame and control, as we are of being caught by the unpredictable in life.

There is much talk in church circles about God being within us, as though He were a possession. There is almost an implication that we are big enough to contain Him, and that He is only part of us. There is even the greater danger of suggesting that we can cage Him or control Him. It would be far more revealing to say that we are in God: 'In Him we live and move and have our being.' It is because we do not venture very far that we do not see that the God who is beyond is also the God who is near at hand. It is when we go out from the safe and secure, when we reach over new boundaries, that we discover the God who is immanent and yet in the beyond. We are ever so afraid to let go, in case we lose control: we are afraid to stretch out in case we cannot return. We need learn to 'let go and let God'. Let Him be the One who controls, for that is facing the reality of the situation. Let Him be the One who comes to meet us in our explorations.

There in the beyond, which is ever reaching to us, we discover a promise of an even yet greater potential, a richness that is still opening out before us. We see with the eye of vision even greater vistas, deeper relationships are waiting to be revealed. So we need to become explorers, that the vision of our world and ourselves may be extended. We need to discover the reality of our existence: to know who we are and to Whom we belong.

One of the great moments of our life is when we

suddenly have our eyes opened, and it is as if we see for the first time. We say with the blind man from St John's Gospel, 'I once was blind but now I see.'[7] Often we do not know how this sight or insight came about, but we do know that our vision has been extended. A prayer by Origen that I like using begins with the words, 'May the Lord Jesus touch our eyes, as He did those of the blind. Then we shall see in the visible things those things which are invisible . . .'

That is something which the Celtic Church seemed to do a lot more easily than we do today – 'to see in the visible things those things which are invisible'. I do not believe that they saw God in all his glory any more than we do, but they certainly saw signs of His Presence. They were aware of creation pointing towards its Creator, and because creation has a Creator we are offered a relationship through it to Him. They saw 'in scenes the unambiguous footsteps of God', to use William Cowper's words. For them, creation was a way of communing with God. Created things spoke to them of the goodness and love of the Creator who was involved in and with His creation. He was not a God who had left it to run itself. So creation was the means of communion with Father, Son and Holy Spirit. Everything spoke of a Presence, vibrated with His love. They saw a universe ablaze with His glory, suffused with a Presence that calls, nods and beckons – a creation personally united with its Creator in every atom and fibre. There was nothing in this creation that need be without, or was without, that glory. Through all things there was a chance of a personal relationship with God.

If it is not so for us, if our vision has become impaired, it is not that we are too materialistic, rather that we are not materialistic enough. We have limited our vision of matter, of God's creation. We need to discover again that there is no separation into sacred and profane. We need to see that all is in God and that God can be seen in all. We need to forever extend our vision beyond that which we seem to set for ourselves. We need to regain a sense of wonder, reverence and awe. Teilhard de Chardin wrote:

Happy the man who fails to stifle his vision . . . What you saw gliding past, like a world, behind the song and behind the colour and behind the eye's glance does not exist just here or there but is a Presence existing equally everywhere: a presence which, though it now seems vague to your feeble sight, will grow in clarity and depth. In this presence all diversities and impurities yearn to be melted away.[8]

Again he said:

God whom we try to apprehend by the groping of our lives – that self-same God is as pervasive and perceptible as the atmosphere in which we are bathed. He encompasses us on all sides, like the world itself. What prevents you, then, from enfolding him in your arms? Only one thing: your inability *to see him*.[9]

This is the great tragedy of so many of us; our vision has become so restricted. One of our difficulties is that we are always wanting to take things apart, to analyse. To dissect living things is fatal! The Celtic Christians tended to seek to discover the underlying unity in things rather than their separation, to align things rather than to divide them. Instead of looking at secondary causes of secondary causes they were concerned with the Prime Mover who united all. There was a consciousness of the integral wholeness in nature, an almost tender awareness of the unseen strands that unite all things and that vibrate with the Presence.

So many of us have lost touch with this reality and

thus live in a fantasy world of distorted vision and great divisions. In this distorted world one can be very alone. This restricted world is of our own making and not half as exciting or interesting as the real thing. What we need to do is to break out from this narrow myopic world and widen our vision. Let us be seen as those who extend horizons, those who reach beyond the stars, beyond the created universe to the Creator Himself, who gives meaning and being to all. Let us look into the very centre of things and discover the mystery that unites all. Let us forever in our looking at material things say, 'Be thou my vision, O Lord.'

In the cartoon world I find Mr Magoo really funny; he is so myopic that he cannot see the end of his nose. Because of his lack of vision he is forever getting into scrapes. His near blindness leads him to all sorts of adventures of which he is unaware. He walks off a building just as a girder comes past, he steps off the girder as it touches the ground. He steps into an open manhole as a head pops out and acts like a stepping-stone. He walks across a lake stepping on the backs of crocodiles, thinking they are logs. His antics are hilarious. But in reality he is tragic; he would cause no end of trouble to himself and to others. In fact he would not survive for long, and neither would people around him. Where there is a lack of vision, life and communities are always endangered. Where vision is lost, people find their lives falling apart. It is of major importance to realise the need for vision and to take seriously the comment from the book of Proverbs: 'Where there is no vision the people perish.'[10]

Our vision of life and the world affects our being as much as our well-being. It is important to us that we have a clear vision of the world and ourselves. I remember once picking up a book entitled, *How to Improve your Vision Without Glasses*. It was a system of daily exercises. I cannot now quite remember the titles of each section but they were something like these:

'How to extend your vision'
'How to see what was once invisible to you'
'How to increase your range'
'Do not miss out on the small things, they are often important'.

I realised that nearly every chapter applied to me, not just to what I could and could not see but to my whole approach to the world. My vision had been far too limited. It reminded me of William Blake, who said: 'If the doors of perception were cleansed everything would appear to man as it is, infinite. For man has closed himself up, till he sees all things thro' narrow chinks of his cavern.'[11] Our world is never big enough to contain God completely; the bigger we see it, or the deeper into it we go, the better chance it has of giving us a glimpse of its Creator.

It is good to make the practical discovery that much of what we call 'spirituality' is in fact how we see. Our spirituality is our vision of the world, ourselves and our Creator. Without the vision of a Creator it is a very small and narrow vision indeed. That is why central to much of Celtic living and prayer is their vision of God, a God in their midst, a God who enfolds, a God incarnate, a God who encompasses the family, a God of the fireside and stable, God in waking and in sleeping.

The Celtic vision derives much of its insight from St John's Gospel, and the symbol of that Gospel is the eagle. The eagle was believed to be able to fly higher than any other bird and to see further. The eagle's vision was able to look deeper and to see beyond others, to see what for others was invisible. This was a very earthy vision, rooted in creation. The vision of the Celts was sacramental rather than mystical: they saw God in and through things rather than by direct visions.

Creation spoke to them of God, conveyed a Presence, because it was in God. When God spoke to them it was usually through His creatures. The Great Other communicated to them through others, through 'mouth of friend and stranger'.

The Celtic Church in its love for St John's Gospel sought to have this vision. They prayed that their eyes might be opened, that all their senses might be made alert to that which was invisible. They prayed that they might have the eagle's eye to see Him who comes at all times. They sought to discover Him in the garden like Mary Magdalene and to be able to say, 'I have seen the Lord.' Like the disciples in the Upper Room, they shared the joy of His Presence in their home, and received His peace. They expected to encounter Him when they were fishing and on the seashore, and they would be sure He shared a meal with them. Time and again they would express their love for Him like Peter and desire to follow Him forever like the Beloved Disciple.[12] They would say in their own words, 'We beheld His glory.'[13] They soared to the heights of awareness and saw deeper than many peoples, for they sought to see with the eye of the eagle.

Not only our vision but all our senses need to be re-educated and re-tuned. We are so used to belonging to a consumer society, which gobbles up one thing after another and savours very little. We need to sharpen our taste for living, and our listening to others. The Celt says we must take time to learn to play the 'five-stringed harp', that is, use all our five senses. Each of our senses can learn to respond to a wider range, and the very centre of our being to be allowed to vibrate to the call of Him who is. As God's world and revelation comes primarily through our senses, we need to be sure they are all functioning as well as can be. A person who is bad at listening to another is not very likely to hear the Great Other who is God. If our vision is narrow then there is no room for the great God. The road to the glory of God is through a reverence for and awareness of the glory that is all about us. If our attitude towards the world – or even towards a single creature – is wrong, then our vision will be distorted and our attitude to God wrong also.

A prayer for the day from Gairloch is about each of our senses:

> Do Thou, O God, bless unto me
> > Each thing mine eye doth see;
> Do Thou, O God, bless unto me
> > Each sound that comes to me;
> Do Thou, O God, bless unto me
> > Each savour that I smell;
> Do Thou, O God, bless unto me
> > Each taste in mouth doth dwell;
> Each sound that goes into my song,
> > Each ray that guides my way,
> Each thing that I pursue along,
> > Each lure that tempts to stray,
> The zeal that seeks my living soul,
> The Three that seek my heart and whole,
> > The zeal that seeks my living soul
> > The Three that seek my heart and whole.[14]

Through our ordinary – God-given – senses the Divine, the Holy Three, seeks out our heart and soul. If our senses are not aware of this they need re-training, until we are aware that we are part of the mystery of Creation. For many this will be like a homecoming. We shall discover that like the prodigal son we have been in a far country and living off poor fare – if not suffering from famine – when in our Father's house there are riches indeed. Like the prodigal we need come to our senses, for here is the road open to God. Let us also seek out our Father and say, *'Be thou my vision.'*

Be Opened

Lord, open our lips,
And our mouth shall declare your praise.

Lord, open our eyes,
And our seeing shall behold your glory.

Lord, open our hearts,
And our feeling shall know your love.

Lord, open our minds,
And our thinking shall discover your wonders.

Lord, open our hands,
And our giving shall show your generosity.

Lord, open our lives,
And our living shall declare your Presence.

Give to me O God
A clear and watchful eye

Give to me O God
A firm but gentle touch

Give to me O God
A good receptive ear

Give to me O God
A clean discerning taste

Give to me O God
A subtle sense of smell

Give to me O God
An openness to others

Give to me O God
An awareness now of you.

With Us

The Lord is here,
His Spirit is with us.

We need not fear,
His Spirit is with us.

We are surrounded by love,
His Spirit is with us.

We are immersed in peace,
His Spirit is with us.

We rejoice in hope,
His Spirit is with us.

We travel in faith,
His Spirit is with us.

We live in eternity,
His Spirit is with us.

The Lord is in this place,
His Spirit is with us.

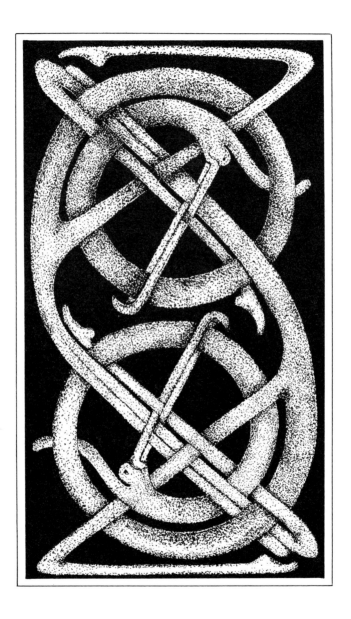

To See Christ

I arise today
Through the strength of Christ's birth with his
*   baptism.*

The Incarnation is a glorious mystery to be enjoyed! In every age it has expressed the love of God for the world, His coming to us and being involved with us. It is the greatest expression of a God who is not far off. Our God is not proud; He comes down and is among us.

That God could take upon Him our flesh and dwell among us will remain for ever beyond our comprehension. As a problem, the Incarnation will never come to a definite conclusion. But that is to do with the limits of our minds and not the limits of God. If we would restrict God to our way of thinking, He must be a very small god indeed.

Many people find it easier to begin with the love of God for us, rather than the birth at Bethlehem. Begin by knowing that God cares for His world and is deeply involved in it. In comprehension He transcends our little minds, but in love He is immanent. God is at hand, waiting to be discovered.

> Lift the stone and you will find me
> Cleave the wood and I am there.

Once you believe and begin to experience the Presence, the Incarnation is then to be seen as yet another way of God's communicating with us. 'The Word was made flesh and dwelt among us, and we beheld His glory.'[15] The coming of God in Christ Jesus is a unique event in all its fullness and it is still the way to the heart of God – through Jesus Christ our Lord.

For many today the way to God is through service, through caring, through loving our brothers and sisters. This can be a way to discover the Incarnation, the Divine in our midst. This is expressed simply, but very well in the little verse:

> I sought my God
> My God I could not see.
> I sought my soul
> My soul eluded me.
> I sought my brother
> And I found all three.

St Martin of Tours influenced the Celtic Church by the form of mission and monastic settlement he helped to establish in Gaul. Here, one of the founding fathers of the Celtic Church, St Ninian, received some of his training. There is no doubt that the vision of St Martin was something the early Church treasured: a vision of 'Christ in friend and stranger'.

Whilst still in the Roman army and preparing to become a Christian, Martin was stationed near Amiens. One cold day, he went out with his soldier companions. They wore heavy cloaks to protect them from the bitter weather. Their cloaks were among their prized possessions. As they approached the city gates, they met a beggar who was near naked and about to perish with the cold. As soon as he saw him, Martin was moved with compassion. He drew his sword and cut his cloak in two, giving one part to the beggar. His companions jeered and mocked him for his foolishness; they would not let him forget such folly in a hurry. That night Martin had a vision. He saw into the kingdom of heaven, and there was Christ surrounded by angels. Christ was wearing the cloak that Martin had given to the beggar. Martin heard Christ say, 'Look, this is the cloak which Martin has given to me this day.' Martin had discovered the great secret of God Incarnate. The Incarnation, though unique in Christ Jesus, is not a past event, but an eternal event. The Incarnation is continuous and is there for us to experience.

Other experiences that are well known are those of St Christopher and St Francis. Christopher struggled across the ford with a child on his shoulders. The child needed help, and Christopher gave it. On reaching the other bank, Christopher put the child down and proceeded to dry himself. During this time the child disappeared – likely went off home. Perhaps in later years Christopher could have put a name to that child, but that night he knew it was Christ! It was from that incident that he took the delightful name of Christ-bearer – Christopher.

St Francis sought to express the love of God in all of creation. This was not too difficult with the birds and the flowers. It was hard when he was confronted with a leper covered in sores. Suddenly, Francis was faced with an outcast from society, scorned and rejected of men. With a great effort, he took the leper in his arms, and then knew that he embraced Christ and Christ embraced him. Each of these saints discovered the sacrament of the Divine Presence in a fellow being: 'Whenever you did this for one of the least important of these brothers of mine, you did it for me!'[16]

The Celtic Church celebrates St Bride's Day in February. There are many legends about her and the Christ child, and I believe they are told to keep us aware of the mystical Presence that comes to us. Here is one of them.

A great famine had come upon the land. The parents of Bride were forced to leave home and go to look for food. The little lass was left to look after the house, with only a 'single stoup of water and a bannock of bread'. There were the usual warnings from parents: to be careful with the food for that was all there was, and not to let any strangers into the house. Late that very night, as the light faded into the gloaming, two travellers came down the lane. One was an old man, the other a maid. It was said that the old man had brown hair and a grey beard; the woman was young and very beautiful. They asked for food and a place to rest. Bride felt sorry for them, but she knew she must obey her parents, and not invite them in. She shared with them her water and her bread, then took them round the back of the house to the barn and helped them make it comfortable. When she returned to the front of the house, there she found the bannock was whole again and the water stoup full. She knew in her heart that she had been dealing with more than mere man. When she looked out again, night had fallen, but the stable was surrounded by a brilliant golden light for *Christ had come to earth*.

Jesus said, 'I was the stranger and you received me in your homes.' The legend of St Bride is about a way of seeing; a way of experiencing 'the Word made flesh'; that we may see Christ in others. There is a Celtic Rune of Hospitality used by the Iona Community and by Kenneth MacLeod which says:

> I saw a stranger at yestere'en.
> I put food in the eating place,
> drink in the drinking place,
> music in the listening place,
> and in the sacred name of
>   the Triune
> He blessed myself and my house,
> my cattle and my dear ones,
> and the lark said in her song
> often, often, often,
> goes the Christ in the stranger's guise.

To be able to make room in your life for another – especially a stranger – is a great gift. We need to teach ourselves to give others our undivided attention. Often we call, 'There is no room at the inn'; no room in our hearts, minds or homes. It is when we open ourselves to the other who comes to us that the great Other also seeks to enter our lives. Jesus still says, 'Where two or three come together . . . I am there.'

To see Christ in others is the beginning of a great adventure: to discover that we do not possess Him, but that He comes and possesses us. We do not have to bring Christ to people to discover His Presence in them. In typical Orthodox fashion, Turgenev describes this experience in one of his prose poems. It is what he experienced in a low-pitched wooden church as a boy. He is surrounded by icons of saints and glowing candles.

> All at once some man came up and stood beside
>   me.
> I did not turn towards him: but at once felt that this
>   man was Christ.
> Emotion, curiosity, awe overmastered me suddenly.
> I made an effort . . . and looked at my neighbour.
> A face like everyone's, a face like all men's faces . . .
> What sort of Christ is this? I thought.
> I turned away. But I had hardly turned my eyes
>   from this ordinary man when I felt again that it
>   was really none other than Christ standing
>   beside me.
> Again I made an effort over myself . . .
> And again the same face, like all men's faces, the
>   same everyday, though unknown, features.
> And suddenly my heart sank, and I came to myself.
> Only then I realised that just such a face – a face
>   like all men's faces – is the face of Christ.[17]

There was one Good Friday when I had a Three Hours' service to take in Middlesbrough. I left home rather late. As I came out of the village of Castleton there was a large hill to climb. As I drove up it, I saw a local man struggling with a railway sleeper; where he was going, I do not know. I sped on my way. The nearer I got to Middlesbrough, the more I was bothered. I had seen a man struggling up a hill with a weight of wood. It was Good Friday. I had seen the Christ and passed Him by! I know that man by name, I meet him still; but I know that in him I also met Christ. 'Whenever you did this for the least important of these . . . you did it for me!'

The Incarnation is about a God who comes, who 'invades' our world and is to be discovered among us. It is not that we possess Him, it is that He possesses us.

Too often the Church talks as if it possessed God, as if it could produce Him at will. With some people, there is a danger of feeling that we can produce Him like a white rabbit from the folds of our coat or from the leaves of a book; that He is something we own and can give to others. It is at such a point that Christ seems to do the vanishing trick! The Church has got caught in an imperialist role, saying to others, 'I have this, and I know what is good for you. Without what I have, you are poor and ignorant – not to forget damned! I have the riches to bring to your poverty, I am the possessor of what you need to receive.' Unfortunately, this has been the approach that destroyed rich cultures and beautiful treasures of other lands. Because we failed to listen to and to see the other, we failed to receive their riches; a wealth of spirituality has been lost to us.

With the Celtic Church it was different. The Celtic Church did not so much seek to bring Christ as to discover Him; not to possess Him, but to see Him in 'friend and stranger'; to liberate the Christ who is already there in all His riches. This is a very difficult way from the imperialist: it is to sit humbly and accept the other who comes to you, to share with him and learn from him. It is not the way of the conqueror, but of the explorer and discoverer.

The ancient poem 'The Lyke Wake Dirge' is about how we respond to others, and that is how we will be judged. The poem is obviously based on Matthew 25. 31–46. Here are four verses:

> If ever thou gavest hosen and shoon
> – Every night and all,
> Sit thee down and put them on;
> And Christ receive thy soul.
>
> If hosen and shoon thou ne'er gavest nane
> – Every night and all,
> The whins shall prick thee to the bare bane;
> And Christ receive thy soul.
>
> If ever thou gavest meat and drink
> – Every night and all,
> The fire shall never make thee shrink;
> And Christ receive thy soul.
>
> If meat and drink thou ne'er gavest nane
> – Every night and all,
> The fire will burn thee to the bare bane;
> And Christ receive thy soul.

The Incarnation involves us in social responsibility. It is a challenge to our way of life. It is in the cry of the poor that Christ still calls to us; in the call of the other that He comes to us.

From the Incarnation – God with us – it is an easy step to baptism, the total immersion into the Father, Son and Holy Spirit. When it comes to baptism, I believe in total immersion, where the person is submerged, surrounded, completely covered. (But parents need not worry when they bring their children to baptism: I am not going to start dipping them in the font, nor am I going to take them down to the river! I will continue the symbolic sprinkling – but it is a symbol of the total immersion.)

Too many people are just sprinkled with Christianity – some would say immunised against the real thing; they have a little bit of faith, a few beliefs, some grasp of the story of Jesus. But it can hardly be called immersion. There are some who dip in now and again, when they feel like it – a strange sort of relationship with their God. It could hardly be called a 'love affair'.

No, I believe in total immersion – none of this half-hearted approach. Even on an everyday level, when the world is going mad and there is trouble all around, it is good to immerse yourself in something sensible like a book or a good play, or to get immersed in garden or sport – so that they involve your whole being. It is amazing how much energy we have to do the things we want to do!

Jesus said, *immerse* people everywhere in the name of the Father and of the Son and of the Holy Spirit. Everywhere, and at all times, immerse people in the Presence of the Creator, the Redeemer, the Strengthener. Like the Incarnation, baptism is not a once-and-for-all event. It is a continuous process. You are not 'done', but forever renewing and re-doing. Like all relationships, to be immersed in the Trinity needs our constant attention and working at. Water baptism is only the beginning of the adventure of total immersion. We must daily, if not hourly, immerse ourselves, our children, our homes, our work, our world in the powers of the Sacred Three. This is not making the relationship happen, but becoming aware that it is a fact: 'we dwell in Him and He in us'.

> *I arise today*
> *Through the strength of Christ's birth with his*
> *baptism.*

We would see Christ

In the birth of a child
In the love of a parent
In the joining of lives
                    We would see Christ.

In the meeting of a friend
In the question of a stranger
In the meeting with another
                    We would see Christ.

In the journey on the train
In the office's routine
In the factory's production
                    We would see Christ.

Total Immersion

Water baptism is not enough; we must totally immerse ourselves, our children and our world in the Sacred Three. Before each verse, we could speak the name of a godchild or loved one.

In the presence of the Father I immerse thee
That to thee He may protecting be
Watching over thy head
Keeping thee from dread
In the presence of the Creator I immerse thee.

In the presence of the Son I immerse thee
That to thee He may a Saviour be
May He keep thee whole and well
Save thee from the jaws of hell
In the presence of the Redeemer I immerse thee.

In the presence of the Spirit I immerse thee
That He may a mighty strengthener be
May He guide thee, lead, empower
Give thee hope in the darkest hour
In the Spirit the life-giver I immerse thee.

In the Holy and blessed Three, I immerse thee
Into their love and joy I place thee
Into their peace and power I steep thee
Into the hands that will keep thee
Into the Trinity of love I immerse thee.

A Genealogy

Son of the elements,
    Son of Vapours
    Son of Wind
    Son of Air.

Son of the elements,
    Son of Light
    Son of Heat
    Son of Fire.

Son of the elements,
    Son of Rain
    Son of Waves
    Son of Water.

Son of the elements,
    Son of Land
    Son of Soil
    Son of Earth.

Son of the elements,
    Son of Stars
    Son of Planets
    Son of Moon.

Son of the elements,
    Son of Creatures
    Son of Man
    Son of God.

Flowing Free

The love of God
Flowing free
The love of God
Flow out through me

The peace of God
Flowing free
The peace of God
Flow out through me

The life of God
Flowing free
The life of God
Flow out through me.

Jesus is Here

Jesus coming down from heaven,
come to me.
Jesus born in a stable,
be born in me.
Jesus accepting the shepherds,
accept me.
Jesus receiving the Magi,
receive me.
Jesus dwelling in Nazareth,
dwell in me.
Jesus abiding with Mary,
abide with me.
Jesus tempted of Satan,
deliver me.
Jesus healing the blind,
give sight to me.
Jesus curing the dumb,
give speech to me.
Jesus light of the world,
enlighten me.
Jesus risen from the dead,
uplift me.

Jesus Son of Mary

Jesus Son of Mary
             be born in us today.
Jesus lost in the Temple
             seek us when we pray.
Jesus living in Nazareth
             make our house your home.
Jesus in desert tempted
             forgive us when we roam.
Jesus making water wine
             fill us with your life divine.
Jesus light upon our way
             ever in our darkness shine.
Jesus healer of the sick
             make us strong and whole.
Jesus betrayed, denied
             protect our body and soul.
Jesus upon the cross
             our sure Saviour be.
Jesus risen from the dead
             give us life eternally.
Jesus, King, Ascended Lord
             evermore by us adored.

In the Beginning, God

PAUSE

Know that at this very moment we dwell in Him, and He
in us.
Our beginning and our end are in Him.
In Him we live and move and have our being.
Know that all things have their beginning in Him.

Rest for a few moments knowing the fact that nothing
can separate us from the love of God.

PICTURE

Meister Eckhart said, 'Every creature is a word of God
and a book about God.'

Take a piece of creation and start to seek out its
beginnings. Take something earthy and discover the
mysteries of creation. See if you can visualise how the
first drop of water began, or how soil was formed over
the earth.

Picture the beginning of the air we breathe, or the
start of a single species of flower. Choose just one thing
and probe its depths, its mysteries and its beginnings.

I seek to meditate every week on a single part of
God's creation. Why not do the same?

PONDER

Take time to consider that –
God is beyond space.
God is beyond time.
God is beyond matter.
God is beyond words.
God is beyond understanding.
God is beyond our senses.

This is what some people call 'transcendence', the God
beyond.

But God is also IN.

> In the beginning, God.
> In the beginning of space.
> In the beginning of time.
> In the beginning of matter.
> In the beginning of our life.
> In his creation.
> In the heart of each of us.

This is what some people call 'immanence', declaring that God is among us and is to be discovered through His creation.

We can see creation as the first incarnation, where God dwells and it is in God. For us the primary scriptures are creation. God is waiting to be revealed through His world. If we fail to understand His world, or decide that we do not like it, how can we understand or love its Creator?

We must seek God in every beginning, for He is there. We must learn to discover His Presence in each encounter. It is how we begin that will influence how we continue and what we see, so we need to begin with the glory and the Presence. We can discover that the God who is beyond can be comprehended by our love and that love of necessity must begin with His world. Here is part of a sermon by the Celtic monk Columbanus:

Seek no farther concerning God: for those who wish to know the great deep must first review the natural world. For knowledge of the Trinity is properly likened to the depths of the sea, according to the saying of the Sage. And the great deep who can find it out? If then a man wishes to know the deepest ocean of divine understanding, let him first if he is able scan that visible sea, and the less he finds himself able to understand of those creatures which lurk beneath the waves, the more let him realise that he can know less of the depths of its Creator: and as he ought and should, let him venture to treat less of Creator than of creature, since none can be competent in the greater if he has not first explored the less, and when a man is not trusted in the lesser, in the greater how should he be trusted? For why, I ask, does a man ignorant of earthly things examine the heavenly? . . . Understand the creation if you wish to know the Creator.[18]

So let us make sure that we do just that; let us seek to comprehend with our love even if we cannot with our mind. It is a pity that, when given the privilege of a mystical revelation through creation, most of us just want to make an inventory. We are a consumer society and we consume rather than savour.

'God's goodness fills all His creatures and all His blessed works full and endlessly overflows in them.'[19]

PROMISE
That each day you will look at one of God's creatures with love and that you will explore its beginnings.

PRAYER
O God of the morning, Christ of the hills,
O Spirit who all the firmament fills,
O Trinity blest who all goodness wills,
        Keep us all our days.[20]

Incarnatus Est

Glory to God on earth peace
Let this song never cease

As I arise this morn
Christ in me be born

When I wash my face
Bless me with your grace

When I comb my hair
Keep me from despair

When I put on my clothes
Your presence Lord disclose

This is the day that you are born
Let every day be a Christmas morn

Glory to God on earth peace
Let this song never cease

New Day

In this world of dark brightness,
Where the night would us enthrall,
I lift my heart to the morning
And to Christ who is Lord of all.

In this world of much trouble,
Where dread things can befall,
I lift my eyes to the sun rising
And to Christ who is Lord of all.

In this world of deep shadow,
Where death will one day call,
I lift my mind to the dawning
And to Christ who is Lord of all.

I lift my life to the morning
And to Christ who is Lord of all,
To eternal life now calling
And the brightness given to all.

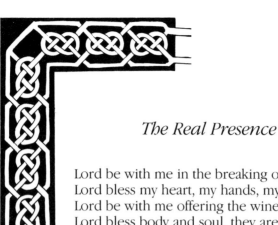

The Real Presence

Lord be with me in the breaking of the bread
Lord bless my heart, my hands, my head
Lord be with me offering the wine
Lord bless body and soul, they are thine.

Lord present in the wine and bread
Stay with me Lord when I am fed
Bless the way by which I go
Guide me in this world below.

Lord thou art there in bread and wine
Around my life may thou entwine
Bless O Lord the life I lead
From sin and stain keep me freed.

Thy Presence come between me
And all things evil
Thy Presence come between me
And all things vile
Thy Presence come between me
And all things of guile
Thy Presence come between me
And all things that defile
Keep me O Lord as the apple of thine eye
Hide me under the shadow of thy wings.

Speak, Lord

In the silence of the stars,
In the quiet of the hills,
In the heaving of the sea,
        Speak, Lord.

In the stillness of this room,
In the calming of my mind,
In the longing of my heart,
        Speak, Lord.

In the voice of a friend,
In the chatter of a child,
In the words of a stranger,
        Speak, Lord.

In the opening of a book,
In the looking at a film,
In the listening to music,
        Speak, Lord,

For your servant listens.

Between Searching
and Knowing

ST MARK

Each Church is Bethlehem

I open the stable door,
I kneel before the infant.
I worship with the shepherds.
I adore the Christ child.
I ponder the Word made flesh.
I absorb the love of God.
I sing Glory with the angels.
I offer my gifts with the Magi.
I have come from lands afar.
I receive the living Lord.
I hold him in my hands.
I go on my way rejoicing,
Glorifying and praising God.

Pathways

Lord, today brings
   Paths to discover
   Possibilities to choose
   People to encounter
   Peace to possess
   Promises to fulfil
   Perplexities to ponder
   Power to strengthen
   Pointers to guide
   Pardon to accept
   Praises to sing
and a Presence to proclaim.

In Heaven Today

I am more in heaven than on earth,
For I am the child that you gave birth.
You made me possessing eternal life,
Let me not lose it by sin or strife.

This is the world which dwells in you,
Open my eyes to know this is true.
All is enfolded, Lord, in your peace;
Let me experience it, and fears cease.

Help me to see that you, Lord, are here;
Then brightness comes and daystars appear.
Grant us to feel you are with us now,
Teach us in wonder before you to bow.

Everything created you, Lord, embrace,
Help us to sense it in this very place,
That we may know that whatever appear,
You, Lord, are present and with us here.

all that they see and know. By itself this one-sided view is very depressing. But thank God there is another side. Experience tells us of this other side; we do have 'infinite longings'. Turn inwards and explore your own being, seek to understand why you are frustrated. In a world so full of things, seek to comprehend what is meant when a teenager says, 'I'm bored.' Seek to explore the 'inner universe' of yourself.

When we look inwards, we discover that we can take in great tracts of the outside world and not be filled or fulfilled. There is a sense in which the whole universe itself cannot satisfy us. Our inner being is itself an expanding universe and finite things do not have the capacity to fill it, for it is made to hold the Eternal. The only real cure for *Angst* is the Eternal. Without God all frustrates: with Him in us the whole world is changed.

The writers of our Scriptures often called our inner being 'the heart'. The heart is not just our feelings or passions, it is meant to describe the very centre of our being. As the heart is almost in the centre of our body and the driving power of our circulation, it is not too far from the truth to look at it as the centre of our life. But it is not just a physical centre, it is that upon which our whole being is based. The words 'heart' and 'soul' can be almost interchangeable as in Psalm 84: 'My soul hath a desire and longing to enter into the courts of the Lord: my heart and my flesh rejoice in the living God.'[4]

Whether it is 'heart' or 'soul' it is obviously the whole person that longs to rejoice in the Presence. The heart is that which makes us essentially who and what we are, it is the very core of our personality and our existence. The Celtic Christians talked of the heart in this way; they saw it as being the very essence of our life. They were familiar with the writings of St Augustine and they knew well the saying: 'Lord, our hearts are restless, until they rest in Thee.' They knew that our relationship to God had to be an affair of the heart, of the very centre of our being. They were aware that we had to be in Him, our hearts had to rest in Him, if we were to find peace.

There is a lovely story of a Hebridean princess which expresses the relationship between God and the heart. The princess was renowned for her gentleness towards all of life. Needless to say such a gentleness is not possible if we are feeling frustrated. She was not possessed by things, and so was able to give much away. She had given food and shelter to one of the wandering saints. Before he left, he asked her,

> 'Tell me the secret of your exceeding gentleness.' At this the lady mused for long, her eyes downcast; then answered softly as one waking from a lovely dream, 'There is no secret – only – only I am always at His feet, and He is always in my Heart.'[5]

This relationship of heart to Heart can be seen again and again in Celtic prayers. There is a wonderful series of morning prayers by a crofter on Morar called Mary Gillies; here are two verses:

> I am giving thee worship with my whole life every
> hour,
> I am giving thee assent with my whole power,
> With my fill of tongue's utterance I am giving thee
> praise,
> I am giving thee honour with my whole lays . . .

> I am giving thee loving with my devotion's whole
> art,
> I am giving kneeling with my whole desire,
> I am giving thee liking with my whole beating of
> heart,
> I am giving affection with my sense-fire;
> I am giving mine existing with my mind and its
> whole,
> O God of all gods, I am giving my soul.[6]

Then there is a prayer that was said at the barring of the door and the putting out of the light. As the darkness descends the speaker puts his trust in God. As the door is barred against evil, as he seeks to close his home to oppression, he opens himself to the Lord of his heart. In this darkness He will be his light. In the silence he is not alone.

> No ill-doing come to me
> Through bar, door-leaf, or turned key;
> No oppression may I see,
> King of glory leading me.
>
> Light of lights take darkness' part
> From thy place into my heart;
> Spirit's wisdom music start
> From my Saviour in my heart.[7]

Not only did the heart find peace and protection through the Presence, the heart was able to sing because of it. Then in turn, by singing, the heart opened itself even more to the Presence. Through song in the heart the world vibrated with the joy of a close relationship with God. One of the things that we know about the Celtic Christians is that they loved to sing; they loved to let the words of their prayers surround them with sound and vibration. This was something very special to them, and they did not share it easily with those who would not understand. They took the Scripture seriously which says 'Sing and make music to the Lord in your heart.' In this resonant harmony every fibre of their being tuned in to the world around them and to their God within the world. They knew, within themselves, that discord was being done away and that all is one in Him.

My mother would be asking us to sing our morning song to God down in the back-house, as Mary's lark was singing it up in the clouds and as Christ's mavis was singing it in yonder tree, giving glory to the God of the creatures for the repose of the night, for the light of the day, and for the joy of life. She would tell us that every creature on the earth here below and in the ocean beneath and in the air above was giving glory to the great God of the creatures and the worlds, of the virtues and of the blessings, and would we be dumb.[8]

As the Lord filled their hearts, He was known to fill the universe. Through such singing, they maintained a feeling of well-being which was truly theirs. A fullness entered lives that knew emptiness: a richness replaced much of the poverty that was their lot. Life was still hard but they were not left to get on alone. Life and creed were one because they were one with Him. This was not so much an intellectual statement as an experience that welled up from their innermost being. There, at the very centre of their life, and at the centre of all things, was their God.

In the Bible there are over nine hundred and sixty references to the heart. There is no one single precise meaning; perhaps this is purposeful if we are talking about the centre of our being. The centre is not something that can be tied down in a living person. Sometimes 'heart' means the will, other times it is the emotions, or the memory, or our personality.

Whatever it linked with it was used to describe the ground of our being. If you enter deep enough into the ground of your being, there you will find the Heart of our own heart. Peter Toon writes:

> Standing before him in the heart suggests an attitude of sincere openness in the very centre of our being, the place where Love creates love; further, the placing of the intellect (mind) in the heart means there is no opposition between mind and heart, for both are open to, and submitted to the Lord God.[9]

When we seek out the core of our existence, if we are not to become self-centred, we need to continue our seeking until we come to God Himself. I know I must not give up until I come to the 'great Heart of my own heart'. Then I will discover that I am in fact in the Heart of God. My love may be small and vacillating, but His for me is great and sure. I will learn that I have always been in my Father's house and heart, and that He has been looking for me with an everlasting love. Life is no longer full of *Angst* which distorts and disturbs my vision. Through the heart relationship, the vision is cleared and all things seem to speak of God. Through the heart being receptive, God is able to approach us through all of His creation.

Bless to me, O God, the moon that is above me.
Bless to me, O God, the earth that is beneath me.
Bless to me, O God, my wife and my children.
And bless, O God, myself who have the care of
   them.

Bless, O God, the thing on which my eye doth rest.
Bless, O God, the thing on which my hope doth rest.
Bless, O God, my reason and my purpose.
Bless, O bless Thou them, Thou God of life.[10]

This common union with God and His creation leads to an awareness of the Kingdom which is within. It teaches us that the Kingdom of God is ever at hand and waiting for us to be receptive to it. If the heart is open to Him, and the will seeks to serve Him 'whose service is perfect freedom', then the Kingdom of God has taken root within us. The Kingdom is always there in potential, waiting for us to accept the rule of the King. Wherever He is loved, wherever He is obeyed, His Kingdom comes on earth as it is in heaven: 'I find Thee throned in my heart, my Lord Jesus. It is enough. I know that Thou art throned in heaven. My heart and heaven are one.'[11]

The deeper discovery than our love for God is His love for us, that we are in the heart of God. Because it is the Almighty who loves us, 'nothing can separate us from the love of God in Christ Jesus'. It is this that allows men to venture on dangerous and troubled seas. When God is in their boat, who are they to fear? In the knowledge of God's love they are not afraid to go anywhere. They know they may never return home, but they are assured of an eternal home. They know they may be lost at sea but they know in their heart they are not lost eternally. Like anyone else they do not want to be separated from their loved ones, yet if it happens they know they will not be separated from the Love of God.

> What can afear
> With God the Father near?[12]

Once again the Celtic fishermen take the Scriptures at their word: 'Let not your hearts be troubled, neither let them be afraid.' The love of God dispels the darkness of fear. The same love is a protection against the storms of life or the greyness of a dull day.

> Though the dawn breaks cheerless on this Isle today, my spirit walks upon a path of light. For I know my greatness. Thou hast built me a throne within Thy heart. I dwell safely within the circle of Thy care.[13]

Once we discover that the centre of our being is centred in God, we discover that we shall not perish. To know we are loved and accepted by God is to know that He will be with us whatever happens. This does not mean we shall escape the storms and tempests of life, but it does mean we are never alone. It also means that, through Him and in Him, we shall not be overcome.

Great Heart of my own heart, whatever befall,
still be thou my vision, thou Ruler of all.

EXERCISES

1. Open up to God. Know that in calling upon Him it is
not that He comes to you, for He is always with you, it is
you opening your heart to Him.

O Lord, my heart is ready,
My heart is ready.

Creator of all, come to me.
Let Your Presence renewing be.
O Lord, my heart is ready,
My heart is ready.

Saviour of all, come to me.
Let Your peace enfolding be.
O Lord, my heart is ready,
My heart is ready.

Spirit of all, come to me.
Let Your power refreshing be.
O Lord, my heart is ready,
My heart is ready.

I come to Thee, Holy Three.
Let me rest myself in Thee.
O Lord, my heart is ready,
My heart is ready.

Know that in your reaching out for God, He comes to
meet you. He has been waiting for you to turn to Him, so
that He may enfold you in His love. He is the great Heart
of your own heart.

2. Pray slowly and carefully:

Almighty God,
to whom all hearts are open,
all desires known,
and from whom no secrets are hidden:
cleanse the thoughts of our hearts
by the inspiration of your Holy Spirit,
that we may perfectly love you,
and worthily magnify your holy name;
through Christ our Lord. Amen.[14]

3. For most of us, the great moment is not so much
when we say we love God but when we realise that God
loves us. Go over these thoughts again and again.

Know that God accepts you whoever you are.
God loves you.
God gives Himself to you.
God is in the very core of your being.

You are in the Presence of God.
You are in the arms of God.
You are in the love of God.
You are in the kingdom of God.
You are in the heart of God.

4. Say quietly and with confidence:

I, Lord, am in your heart.
Your Presence enfolds me.
Your Presence is Love.

As we are in God, we are in His love, His peace, His
power. Let us learn to pray the above prayer many times
a day, changing the final word to whatever of God's gifts
we feel we need. Know that in His Presence these gifts
are offered to you.

Christ the Giver

If Christ be in your heart
Glory fills your days
For He is the King of Glory.

If Christ be in your mind
Peace is in all your ways
For He is the Prince of Peace.

If Christ be in your deeds
Joy your life will raise
For He is the Giver of Joy.

If Christ be in your will
Strength of purpose stays
For He is Sender of Strength.

Full Tide

The full tide is the summer of our lives, a time of depth and growth. It is the time when we achieve much and shape who we are. We seek to enjoy life and live it to the full. We will pass exams and pass many milestones. It is a time for stretching and journeying; a time of opportunities and success. We could hardly talk of this tide without remembering the words of Shakespeare:

> There is a tide in the affairs of men,
> Which, taken at the flood, leads on to fortune;
> Omitted, all the voyage of their life
> Is bound in shallows and in miseries.[15]

Yet, we must realise that the flood tide can also overwhelm and destroy. There are lives that let so much flow in that they are unable to accept anything new; people who are always too busy and have no time. There is a great danger of justifying our lives by hyperactivity, or by how much we have amassed. We need to be aware that this tide will turn also; it is just one of many tides. We may be fortunate enough to have a life that is 'all on flood', but one day at last it must ebb. In our very riches we must make space so that we can experience the deeps that are offered to us. At flood time there is a great depth to be explored, not just a surface to be skimmed. We are not called just to be inshore sailors, but to launch out, and to explore the mysteries of the depths. We approach the great mystery of God through the deep mysteries of His creation, through a reverence for and a respect of the world in which we live.

Full tide in particular is a time of love in all its fullness. If we do not love the creation, how can we say we love its Creator? Some good advice on our approach to life in its fullness comes from Dostoevsky in *The Brothers Karamazov*:

> Brothers, do not be afraid of contact with sinful men. Love man even in his sin, for that love is like the divine love – the highest of all. Love all God's creation – the whole of it, every grain of sand. Love every leaf, every ray of light. Love the animals, love the plants, love everything. If you love each thing you will perceive the mystery of God in all. Once you perceive this, you will begin to understand it better every day, and you will come at last to love the whole world with an all-embracing love.
>
> Brothers, love is a great teacher; but we must learn how to acquire it, for it is got with difficulty. We buy it dearly, slowly, and with much labour. Everyone can love occasionally – even the wicked can do that; but we must love not for a moment but for ever.

To me this sounds like good Eastern Orthodox teaching on meditation. It is also very like the approach of the Celtic Church to nature. If you want further guidelines on this way of looking at the world in its flood, you could hardly find better than Ignatius Loyola's 'Contemplation for achieving love':

> See God in his creatures –
> in matter giving it existence,
> in plants giving them life,
> in animals giving them consciousness,
> in men giving them intelligence.
> So He lives in me, giving me existence, life, consciousness, intelligence . . .
>
> Think of God energising, as though He were actually at work, in every created reality, in the sky, in matter, plants and fruits, herds and the like . . .
>
> Realise that all gifts and benefits come from above. My moderate ability comes from the supreme Omnipotence on high, as do my sense of justice,

kindliness, charity, mercy and so on ... like sun-beams from the sun or streams from their source.[16]

If we are able to begin to approach life like that, we shall be greatly enriched in the flood tide.

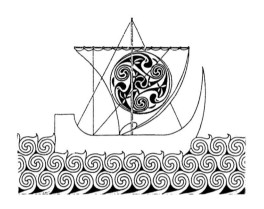

Dedication

I give my hands to you Lord
I give my hands to you

I offer the work I do Lord
I offer the work I do

I give my thoughts to you Lord
I give my thoughts to you

I give my plans to you Lord
I give my plans to you

Give your hands to me Lord
Give your hands to me

Let your love set me free Lord
Let your love set me free

Keep me close to you Lord
Keep me close to you.

Be all else but naught to me, save that thou art.

———

The world and time have a habit of bringing all things to nought. There is a sense in which nothing seems to endure. There is something about nature and the human being which does not last. This is expressed in the Psalms in such a phrase as 'God bringeth all men to nought'. The poet Shelley describes a fallen statue in the desert, with these words on its pedestal:

> 'My name is Ozymandias, King of Kings:
> Look on my works, ye Mighty and despair!'
>
> Nothing beside remains. Round the decay
> Of that colossal wreck, boundless and bare
> The lone and level sands stretch far away.[17]

In a world where dangers were all around, the Celtic saints realised more than many the fragility of things. They knew the dangers of travelling through mountain passes and over uncharted seas. They had few of the protections that the modern city dweller pulls around him, so they were more aware that all things come to nought. Even today this feeling of things not lasting is part of the Celtic heritage.

There is something in human nature that makes us all seekers. Whatever we achieve, we feel that we should be able to go on to other things. None of us can live for long off past glories. Most of us have this feeling that life can be improved on. We seek something that is still beyond us, an inner urge makes us explorers. Once we cease from exploration there is a feeling that life is beginning to atrophy. T. S. Eliot writes:

Old men ought to be explorers
Here and there does not matter
We must be still and still moving
Into another intensity
For a further union, a deeper communion
Through the dark cold and the empty desolation,
The wave cry, the wind cry, the vast waters
Of the petrel and the porpoise . . .[18]

The quest for the beyond, for the Pearl of Great Price,
for the Holy Grail, for hidden treasures, is part of the
literature of all mankind: the symbols may differ but the
quest remains the same. In nearly every quest there is a
desert to cross or a jungle to conquer, there are always
untold dangers. Such a venture calls for heroes; in the
end the villains are always sorted out! It is in searching
that we grow, in triumphing over the desert that we
shape ourselves and show what we are made of. When
there were still other countries to be discovered, many
spent their energies doing just that; the quest was
geographical exploration. Today the quest has moved
to outer space. But what does it profit us gaining a
foothold on another planet if we have not explored and
understood our own inner being? The danger with
questing simply after territory is that we carry to it all
that is within us; we take to the new place all our
restlessness and our destructive urges. Tacitus saw this
in the first century: 'They make a desert and they call it
peace.'[19]

There is a noughting, a desert that we all carry within
us. No matter what we put into this desert place, we still
suffer from dryness, from a longing to quench our
insatiable thirst. This desert seeks to grow, and en-
croach on all the territories we know. Some people
carry it around like a great 'black hole', and anything
that comes in reach is swallowed up and diminished –

sadly, there is very little that comes out of them alive. This desert or emptiness needs filling, or one day we will just become part of it; it will spread into all our life.

There certainly is a desert that is simply destructive. But there is also a desert that is creative, a place of transition, which needs to be crossed if we are to leave the old behind. Before the Promised Land is reached there are deserts to cross, before the Pearl of Great Price is obtained we have to sell all that we have. The Old Testament tells the story of desert people, and how in the wilderness places they found refreshment. In the desert Jacob had his dream of the Presence; Moses found the holy ground of the burning bush. The journey from slavery to freedom involves crossing the desert:

> Remember how Yahweh your God led you for forty years in the wilderness, to humble you, to test you and know your inmost heart ... He made you feel hunger ... Learn from this that Yahweh your God was training you as a man trains his child.[20]

In the New Testament, the wise men crossed the desert to come to Jesus. John the Baptist chose the desert as the birthplace of his ministry. Of Jesus, St Mark says that 'the Spirit drove him out into the wilderness and he remained there for forty days, and was tempted by Satan. He was with wild beasts, and the angels looked after him.'[21]

It is good to notice that it is the Spirit who leads Jesus into the desert, for the desert can be a positive place. Once emptied of any trivial pursuits – or false directions – there is a chance for a space to be made for God to work. The desert can be a place where life blossoms, but it is not a place to ignore. When we are unwilling to enter the desert, in a strange way the desert enters us. The deserts of the world are growing; a new aridity and dryness is entering into the hearts and souls of civilised people. If we refuse to empty ourselves, it is often because we are already afraid of the growing emptiness within. We feel we could not survive if we discovered that our inner being was in fact a nothingness or moving towards nothing. But it is when we fear the desert, that we are unable to venture; we put off the Promised Land to another age and another time. We are unable to enter into the heritage that is rightly ours and are forced to sing of a happy land that is 'far far away'. We dare not let go of what we have and so we remain impoverished.

Those who willingly enter the desert may discover with Moses that God is truly present, that the very ground of the desert is holy ground. Those who do not run away discover that

> The desert will rejoice,
>   and flowers will bloom in the wilderness.
> The desert will sing and shout for joy;
>   it will be as beautiful as the Lebanon Mountains
>   and as fertile as the fields of Carmel and Sharon.
> Everyone shall see the Lord's greatness and
>   power . . .
> Streams of water will flow through the desert;
>   the burning sands will become a lake,
>   and dry land will be filled with springs . . .
> There will be a highway there;
>   called 'The Road to Holiness' . . .[22]

It was this knowledge, that the desert could be an exciting place of discovery, that drove many of the Celtic saints out of their homeland. These men and women saw that they had to make space for God, or they were aware that God was forever making such a space and if they did not let Him fill it nothing else was able to do it fully.

Time and time again in the *Voyage of Brendan* we hear of saints who set out to 'find a wilderness in the ocean', a desert place where they could be alone and without all the normal supports. A place where God could be allowed to fill every moment of their day. A place where they could discover that the very earth they walked on is holy, and so in turn know that every place belongs to God. Such a place is Skellig Michael, a remote rock in the Atlantic, the peak of a mountain that sticks 210 metres out of the ocean, seven and a half miles from the coast of Ireland. On this barren land, hardly approachable in most weathers, beehive cells were built where their inhabitants might discover the holy ground in the wilderness. Let those who visit such places on a fine day in summer not romanticise them; these truly were, and are, testing places. Only true heroes or heroines could survive there for long. Only those who are content with God can be satisfied in the wilderness. Once God is known to be there and to be met, the desert blossoms.

This tradition of seeking a 'wilderness' was one of the regular actions of Celtic saints. Bede tells how St Cedd in AD 659 '... chose a site for the monastery among some high and remote hills, which seemed more suitable for the dens of robbers and haunts of wild beasts than for human habitation'. In the same tradition St Cuthbert went to the Inner Farne for the first time in 675. 'Now the island had no water, corn or trees, and being the haunt of evil spirits was very ill-suited to human habitation. But when the man of God came, he ordered the evil spirits to withdraw, and the island became quite habitable.'[23] In 669 St Guthlac left the monastery at Repton for the wild and undrained quagmire of Crowland. His biographer Felix tells us he chose 'a place which many men had attempted to inhabit, but could not settle on account of manifold horrors and fears, and the loneliness of the wide wilderness'.

It is interesting to find how many little places in Celtic lands are called 'Disert', 'Dyserth' or something similar, each describing a place where someone sought to be alone to reach or discover an ideal: all such places were the scene of spiritual battle or adventure – places where someone was willing to face the noughting of the world to find the glory of the Presence. These are places where beauty is found, great and lasting beauty. For until we find Him, we do not know where true beauty is. Beauty without God is also a thing that comes to nought. The true beauty that endures, is a Beauty that is found within.

The desert is not an escape from the world. Those who go to it to run away will bring their own demons with them. It is not the desert-dweller, or the pilgrim for the love of Christ, who is the escapist – it is far more often the tourist! Fewer and fewer places are available to escape to, there are fewer empty spaces and un-crowded shores than ever before. Every year another splendid hide-away is discovered and marketed, and so destroyed. In parts of our world we have destroyed peaceful villages and quiet islands forever by marketing them as places to escape to. To the perpetual tourist here are some salutary words from Seneca:

How can you wonder your travels do you no good, when you carry yourself around with you? You are saddled with the very thing that drove you away. How can novelty of surroundings abroad and becoming acquainted with foreign scenes and cities be any help? All that dashing about turns out to be quite futile. And if you want to know why this running away cannot help you, the answer is simply this: you are running away in your own company. You have to lay aside the load on your spirit. Until you do that, nowhere will satisfy you.[28]

So even the Stoic Seneca could see and experience the noughting of all places. He knew that if a person carried around a desert within, they would find it wherever they went.

St Antony of Egypt said: 'For the sake of Greek learning men go overseas . . . but the city of God hath its foundation in every seat of human habitation . . . the Kingdom of God is within.'[25] The desert fathers were not escapists. Anyone who thinks the desert is an escape should try it!

> The simple men who lived their lives out to a good old age among the rocks and sands only did so because they had come into the desert to be themselves, their ordinary selves, and to forget a world that divided them from themselves. There can be no other valid reason for seeking solitude or for leaving the world.[26]

In the main the desert fathers were not mystics, they were practical men, who organised themselves into what we would call co-operatives and took their surplus produce by boat to market. But, they made a definite decision not to be caught up in the decadent values of their times. Society is ever bent on conventional and transient values, it measures by material standards. It is hard to be your own true self if you are trapped in the perpetual round of doing what is expected of you. It is hard to be measured by worldly standards unless you have 'gained' or 'possessed' something. We find it hard to begin to understand that 'to become the greatest we have to become the least.' If we are to discover our hidden treasure, we have to be willing to let go of all else – 'Naught be all else to me save that Thou art.' Let us show that we believe our God is the God who created out of nothing, and risk welcoming the emptiness. If we accept that God brings goodness and order out of chaos, we should be less afraid to venture. But also, let us be clear about our quest: to give up something for something far better should hardly be called sacrifice. If the quest is for the Pearl of Great Price, then it is worth selling what we have to get it. Let the world see that we are not so much giving up as choosing a better way. The words of St Antony that moved Augustine of Hippo should still have their effect on us: 'Let no one who has renounced the world think that he has given up some great thing . . . The whole earth set over against heaven's infinite is scant and poor.'

What the desert fathers and the Celtic saints did show was a richness of spirit amid their material poverty, a great sense of the eternal present in the passing of things transitory. They showed great poise at a time when many were falling apart. They carried within them a 'rest', an inner calm for which they became famous. This inner calm, *quies*, is about the peace that the world cannot give, the peace that passes all understanding, the peace that is a gift which comes with the Presence of God. They heeded and trusted the call, 'Come unto me and I will give you rest.' It was not an escape from the storms of life, but a witness to the fact that we are not expected to face them alone. They sought to acknowledge that, whatever the troubles which beset us, we are not left alone nor forsaken. Far from being a place of impoverishment, the place of emptying can become the place where we are enriched. It is here that we can discover true and lasting values, and more important, here that we come to rely on our God. Instead of being the place of frantic searching, it can be the place of rest and renewal.

We need to create the space that allows for the Divine, to make room in our lives, as the innkeeper made room in the stable – or He will be born elsewhere. It is only if we are willing to be alone with the Beloved that we can say we truly love Him. This will not decrease our love for the world for it is His creation; it will enhance it. It will not make us love our neighbours less, for we will see Him in them, and so respect them all the more. It will not diminish us as people but fulfil and enrich us. To leave behind all material things is to show that we want the heart-to-Heart encounter, and at the same time it shows that we know where our true riches lie.

Remember, it is the Spirit who leads us into the wilderness. He calls us to where He can court us to love Him: 'I am going to take her into the desert again: there I will win her back with words of love.'[27] Make space daily in your life, times of emptiness for Him to fill, times of silence to heed His call. Know that

> God our pilgrimage impels
> To cross sea-waste or scale life-fells;
>> A further shore,
>> One hill-brow more,
> Draws on the feet, or arm-plied oars,
> As the soul onward, upward soars.
>
> Beyond the hills a wider plain,
> Beyond the waves the Isle domain
>> With richness blest
>> A place for guest,
> Where God doth sit upon his throne,
> The soul by Christ nor left alone.[28]

In whatever situation you find yourself, learn to say these words of love:

Be all else but naught to me, save that thou art.

EXERCISES

1. Make definite spaces in your day; stop all that you are
doing and pray quietly and slowly:

Drop thy still dews of quietness
till all our strivings cease;
take from our souls the strain and stress,
and let our ordered lives confess
the beauty of thy peace.

Breathe through the heats of our desire
thy coolness and thy balm;
let sense be dumb, let flesh retire;
speak through the earthquake, wind and fire,
O still, small voice of calm.

J. G. Whittier

2. PAUSE, PRESENCE, PICTURE, PONDER, PROMISE

PAUSE
Stop all that you are doing. Let yourself relax. See if you
can feel the tension going out of your body as you let go.
Gently put all troubled and anxious thoughts from your
mind. Make a space in your life for something to happen
. . . Make room for God.

Breathe slowly and deeply.
Know He offers you His peace . . . accept it freely.
Let go . . . and let God.

PRESENCE
Know that He is with you.
Speak to Him quietly and say,

You Lord are in this place
Your Presence fills it
Your Presence is Peace.

You Lord are in my heart
Your Presence fills it
Your Presence is Peace.

There is no need to do anything. Just accept that He is
  there.
Rest in His Presence as you would in the sunshine.
Immerse yourself in His peace and in His love.

PICTURE
Picture the scene from Psalm 42.1–2.
The young gazelle travelling the desert places, searching, seeking for water. This has become her over-riding
purpose: without finding it she will die. She must not
weaken or give up in her search. Picture the finding, the
life-saving waters. See her drink deeply. See how she
revives. Know that you are like this and say:

> Like as the hart desires the water-brooks: so longs
>   my soul after thee, O God.
> My soul is athirst for God, yea even for the living
>   God: when shall I come to appear before the
>   Presence of God?[29]

PONDER
How long do you think that you can survive without
coming to Him who is the living water?
Think about the dry and arid areas of your life and know
that God is calling you through them.

PROMISE
That every day this week you will seek Him out.
That if any dry or arid spells come along when you feel
like nothing, you will especially call upon Him.

3. Know that in your desires for change God is at work,
and that God is seeking you more than you are seeking
Him.
Maria Boulding invites you to discover this:

> All your love, your stretching out, your hope, your thirst,
> God is creating in you so that he may fill you. It is not
> your desire that makes it happen, but His. He longs
> through your heart.[30]

An Oblation

I place my hands in yours Lord
I place my hands in yours

I place my will in yours Lord
I place my will in yours

I place my days in yours Lord
I place my days in yours

I place my thoughts in yours Lord
I place my thoughts in yours

I place my heart in yours Lord
I place my heart in yours

I place my life in yours Lord
I place my life in yours

All that I am I give you Lord
All that I am I give you

All that I have I share with you Lord
All that I have I share with you

All my life is yours Lord
All my life is yours

All my desires are yours Lord
All my desires are yours

All my hopes are in you Lord
All my hopes are in you

All I want is you Lord
All I want is you

In Him we Live

Christ with me, Christ before me, Christ behind me,
Christ in me, Christ beneath me, Christ above me,
Christ on my right, Christ on my left,
Christ when I lie down, Christ when I sit down,
   Christ when I arise,
Christ in the heart of every man who thinks of me,
Christ in the mouth of every one who speaks of me,
Christ in the eye of every one that sees me,
Christ in every ear that hears me.

It has been said that Christianity has not been tried and found wanting, it has never been tried. There are few who take Christ fully at His words: 'I will be with you always, to the end of the age.'[31] Because of this, words are used without meaning, ideas without experience. Christ is treated like a person in a book and in history, rather than as the Living Lord. Because there is no real encounter, we dispense with Him as we would dispense with any other idea, and we are left impoverished.

Patrick lived in awareness of the Presence, sure that Christ was with him and in him. That is faith. Faith can be seen as an act of appropriation, of taking to oneself the reality which others only talk of. Faith occurs when we have a personal encounter with God. Then Christ is no longer treated as a historical character but as the one who comes now: present in the Presence. He stands at the door and knocks. He is close to each of us and ready to answer our call. For us, this is the exciting discovery: 'In Him we live and move and have our being.' We are not people of a book, not even of the Bible, but of the Word, the living Christ. A poem by the seventeenth-

century German mystic known as Angelus Silesius
warns us:

> Though Christ a thousand times
> In Bethlehem be born,
> If He's not born in thee,
> Thou art still forlorn.
>
> The cross on Golgotha
> Will never save thy soul,
> The cross in thine own heart
> Alone can make thee whole.

Often, in church, when I turn towards the congregation and say, 'The Lord be with you', I hear a very subdued, even dull reply, 'And also with you'. I proclaim, 'The Lord is here,' and there is hardly a glimmer of excitement. Then I wonder what we are doing and saying. To declare the Presence of our God is one of the most exciting things that we can ever do. Every time we declare the Presence, we should thrill with excitement, our hearts should burst with joyful alleluias. If it has become merely a repetitive and dull statement, we should ask ourselves, 'What has happened to us?' To know the Presence can never be dull; if we are dull it is because we are out of touch. We must stop talking about Him; stop searching for Him in books and distant places, and learn that He has already found us and is within. An old Irish quatrain says:

> Going to Rome? Going to Rome?
> 'Twill bring no profit, only trouble,
> The King thou there would quest
> Not found shall be, if he go not in thy breast.[32]

St Augustine's very moving expression of this discovery speaks for us all at some time:

> Too late have I loved Thee, O Beauty, so ancient yet

ever new, too late have I loved Thee! Lo! Thou wast within and I without, and there I mis-shapen was running in search of Thee amidst those lovely shapes which Thou hadst formed. Thou wast with me, and I was not with Thee . . . Thou didst call, shout, shatter my deafness; Thou didst flash, shine, scatter my blindness. And I drew in my breath and I pant for Thee, I tasted Thee and I hunger and thirst. Thou didst touch me and I burned for Thy peace.[33]

The same Christ is still passing by; it is only our blindness that prevents us from seeing Him. He is ready to hear us and to come to us. We must not be put off by the things that crowd in upon us. Day by day we need to call upon His Presence. We need to shout out like Bartimaeus: 'Jesus! Son of David! Take pity on me.'[34] We need to learn the 'Jesus Prayer'; to call often on His name, for the Lord is at hand. Patrick had obviously learned such a prayer when he called upon the Lord several times in a day. Perhaps in this section of his Hymn we get a glimpse not of one prayer, but of many prayers – short affirmations of the Presence at all times. We, too, need to stop talking about Him and to talk to Him.

Christ with me

Christ, this is not a request but a fact.
You, Christ, are here and with me now.
Christ, open my eyes to Your Presence
        open my ears to Your call,
        open my heart to Your love,
        open my will to Your command.

Christ, you have promised You will be with me 'always, to the end of the age'. My imagination may fail, but Your

Presence is real. My eyes may be dim, but You are still there.

Christ, I call upon your Name, for You are with me. I am never alone, never without help, never without a friend, for I dwell in You and You in me! 'Yea, though I walk through the valley of the shadow of death, I will fear no evil; for You are with me.'

Christ before me

Christ, You have gone before me to prepare a place for me, that where You are, I may be also. There is nowhere I can journey that You have not travelled:

> If I went up to heaven, you would be there;
> if I lay down in the world of the dead, you would
>   be there.
> If I flew away beyond the east,
>   or lived in the farthest place in the west,
>   you would be there to lead me,
>   you would be there to help me.[35]

Christ, I do not know what lies ahead, but I do know *Who* is with me.

Christ, I do not know where I shall end up, but I know *Who* is there before me.

Christ, the future is not fully unknown for You are there before me.

Christ behind me

Christ, You are behind me to protect me from evil, defending me from all that would creep up on me. You stand between me and all that seeks to defile me.

Christ, You enter through the door of the past with Your love and forgiveness. You can come where doors are closed and bring light and peace.

Christ, I put my hand in Yours, for I am afraid; I bring memories that hurt and a past that pains, for Your healing and renewal.

Christ, come enter through the door of the past;
> into the remembered and the forgotten,
> into the joys and sorrows,
> into the recording room of memories,
> into the secret room of sin,
> into the hidden room of shame,
> into the mourning room of sorrow,
> into the bright room of love,
> into the joyful room of achievement.

Come Christ, enter
> into the fibre of our being
> into the conscious and sub-conscious,
> into the roots of personality.

'Cleanse me from my secret faults and renew a right spirit within me.'

Christ in me

Christ, there is no need for long pilgrimages, for You are within. Christ, help me to make the journey inwards and discover Your Presence in me. In this alone is there any dignity that will last. You, O Christ, have chosen to be born in me.

> Christ born in a stable
> is born in me.
> Christ accepted by shepherds
> accepts me.

Christ receiving the wise men
receives me.
Christ revealed to the nations
be revealed in me.
Christ dwelling in Nazareth
You dwell in me.

Christ, grant that people may look at me and see Your Presence.
Christ, help me to know that I am called to be the body of Christ.

Christ has no hands but our hands
To do His work today.
Christ has no feet but our feet
To speed men on their way.
Christ has no lips but our lips
To tell men why He died.
Christ has no love but our love
To win men to His side.

Christ, may Your work be fulfilled in us, and Your Presence revealed in us.

Christ beneath me

Christ, no matter how far I have fallen, You are there also; 'Underneath are the everlasting arms.'

Christ, I look at the hands that uphold me and I see the print of nails. The hands that bear me up know pain and sorrow. You, Lord, know the betrayals and rejections of this world.

Christ, 'if I descend into hell You are there also.' You experienced the many hells of this world. You have descended so that You can lift us up. In all dangers, You are there to support us:

In the storms of life,
In the sinking of the disciple,
In the scorning and rejecting,
In the betrayals and denials,
In the hells and crucifixions,
In the ebbing out of life,
Christ beneath me.
And I know that You are the Risen Lord of Life.

Christ above me

Christ, risen and ascended Lord.
Christ, above all things, You came down to lift us up.
Christ, I know that You walk with me in the storms, and
yet in a strange way You are above the waves.
Christ, I will not sink if You will lift me up.
Christ, as You have ascended, help me also in heart and
mind to ascend and with You dwell forever.

When waves roar and winds increase,
Lift me, Christ, to Your peace.
When the way is dark and the night cold,
Keep me, Christ, in Your hold.
My faith is weak, my vision dim,
Save me, Christ, I cannot swim.
Let Your hand reach down to me,
Lift me from this perplexity.
Ascended Christ, with mighty hand,
Bring me safe again to land.

Christ on my right

Christ with all who are dexterous, all creators and beautifiers of our world.

Christ with all artists and craftsmen, all who enrich our lives working for the good of creation.

Christ in all that comes to life this day, all that grows, blossoms, increases.

Christ in all that is peaceful, joyful and hopeful.

Christ revealed in glory.

Christ in whoever approaches me from the right.

Christ in my neighbour, Christ in hearts of all that love me.

Christ, whoever is at my right. You are in them.

Christ on my left

Christ, there with the sinister, seeking to save.

Christ there with all that would seek to diminish, destroy this day, with all who are burdened and heavy laden.

Christ with all whose lives are drained and emptied this day, with the suffering and poor, the oppressed and the tyrannised.

Christ with all who will die this day.

Christ in whoever approaches me from the left.

Christ in the stranger. Christ in those who rise against me.

Christ to be discovered in all who oppose or hate me.

Christ in all who hinder and exhaust me.

Christ, whoever is at my left. You are in them.

Christ when I lie down

Christ, I come to You when I am weary and heavy laden knowing that You will refresh me. When life lays me low, You will lift me up. 'I will lay me down in peace . . . for it is Thou, Lord, only that makest me dwell in safety.'[36]

> I am going now into the sleep,
> Be it that I in health shall wake;
> If death be to me in deathly sleep,
> Be it that in thine own arm's keep.
> O God of grace, to new life I wake,
> O be it in thy dear arm's keep,
> O God of grace, that I shall awake.
>
> Be my soul on thy right hand, O God,
> O Thou King of the heaven of heaven;
> Thou it was who didst buy with Thy blood,
> Thine the life for my sake was given;
> Encompass Thou me this night, O God,
> That no harm, no mischief be given.[37]

Christ, watch me while I sleep. Let me learn to trust in You.

> Watch thou, dear Lord, with those who wake, or watch, or weep tonight, and give thine angels charge over those who sleep. Tend thy sick ones, O Lord Christ. Rest thy weary ones. Bless thy dying ones. Soothe thy suffering ones. Pity thine afflicted ones. And for all thy love's sake.[38]

Christ when I sit down

Christ when I cease activity,
Christ when I quieten the mind,
Christ when I still the tongue,
Christ when I calm the heart,
Christ in quiet,
Christ, teach me to be still and know that You are
   God.

Christ when I sit down at table,
Christ the uninvited guest,
Christ when I sit down alone, my companion and
   friend,
Christ when I sit down in company – where two or
   three are gathered, You are there.
When I sit down in conference,
Christ in mouth of friend and stranger.

Christ when I arise

Christ when I arise to the new day,
Christ when I arise to the new opportunity,
Christ when I arise above temptation,
Christ when I arise above the storms,
Christ when I arise from all that would depress me,
Christ when I arise from death,
Christ when I arise to Your Presence.

Thanks be to Thee ever, O gentle Christ,
That Thou has raised me freely from the black,
And from the darkness of last night
To the kindly light of this day.[39]

Christ in the heart of every man who thinks of me

Christ, You are to be found in my loved ones.

Christ, help me to set out on the voyage of discovery that he who loves is born of God and knows God. The discovery that as I do it to the least of these, I do it to You.

Christ, let me see Your call in the call for love, in the plea of the poor and needy.

Christ, when we truly love, we open our lives not only to another but to that Great Other which is You.

Christ in the heart of every man, even those who as yet do not know or love You, help me to seek You and in others to find You.

Christ in mouth of every one who speaks of me

'Christ in mouth of friend and stranger.'
Christ, make me attentive to the word, that I may hear the Word.
Christ, make me listen to the other, that I may hear the Other.
Christ, when words fail and communication breaks down, You are still there to keep us together.
Christ, when two or three are gathered together in conversation, You are there.
Christ, speak to me in the voice of a friend, in the chatter of a child, in the words of a stranger.

Christ in the eye of every one that sees me

Christ, let me see You in others.
Christ, let others see You in me.
Christ, let me see:

You are the caller
You are the poor
You are the stranger at my door.

You are the wanderer
The unfed
You are the homeless
With no bed.

You are the man
Driven insane
You are the child
Crying in pain.

You are the other who comes to me
Open my eyes that I may see.

Christ, grant that in me others may see

Your glory,
Your grace,
Your goodness,
Your Presence,
For without You, I am nothing.

Christ in every ear that hears me

Christ, You are there before I speak,
        Help me to respect You.
Christ, You are present in the listener,
        Let me reveal You, or be revealed to me.
Christ, may my words not hide
        You the Word.

    Christ is here,
    Christ is there,
    Christ is everywhere.
    Christ above,
    Christ below,
    Christ along the path I go. Alleluia. Amen.

Launch out into the Deep

Use this time to thrust out a little from the land, to discover the amazing depth of the ordinary. Use it until you discover the extra-ordinary that lies in the depths of all things. Realise that you live in the depths all of your life; life is only shallow when we choose to make it so. Move away from what you do out of necessity and habit. Discover the deeps of creation, of your own being, and of God.

PICTURE

See the fishermen mending their nets. Look at the weariness upon them. They are on the beach and their boats are beached also. It is as if the tide has left them all behind. Their nets are broken and they have taken them into their hands. Great holes that let life slip through have to be repaired. At the moment it seems that life is escaping from them, slipping through the net and through their fingers. They know it is necessary to make the holes smaller. If the mesh is too large, everything will escape them, so they are mending their nets.

It is at such a moment that He comes. He comes when life seems to be escaping us. He comes when we toil all night and get nothing for it. Beware, He is wanting to cast His net and He is making the casting area smaller. He does not want everyone just to slip away. See Him being jostled by the crowds. The beach is becoming so crowded, He can hardly move. If He is to land a great catch like this He will need help. So He calls to the fishermen. He wants their support. He needs a little space. So He borrows their boat – and the fishermen. For a while the talking goes on but then Jesus comes to the important bit: 'Thrust out a little from the land' – a simple request, but it is the beginning of something bigger. It is nice being there with Him, a bit of time off from work. Sitting there and enjoying the gentle movement of the boat. They begin to wonder why they do not do this more often. It is so relaxing, so refreshing. Because of this action they feel especially close to Him. He is in their boat – and in their lives.

'Launch out into the deep!' That order comes as a bit of a shock. It seems that privileges always bring with them responsibilities. They were just beginning to lie back. 'Launch into the deep!' He wants them to be in the deep waters. He knows that big catches are not in these shallows. 'Launch out into the deep and let down your net for a catch.' Peter wanted to object but he also wanted to plumb new depths, so he obeyed. Here was a catch like never before; though the fishermen were not quite sure who was catching what or whom. All Peter knew was that they had entered the deep with Jesus and their lives would never be the same again. Peter knew that when they came down to earth, when they came to land, they were caught. See what new depths they enter as they leave all behind and follow Him.

PONDER

>   Jesus calls us o'er the tumult
>   Of our life's wide restless sea.

While we are doing our routine work, He comes.
While we are mending our nets or our cars, He
    comes.
While the very life we seek is slipping through our
    fingers, He comes.
When we toil all night and catch nothing,
    He comes.
When we are tired and frustrated, He comes.
And every time He comes, He calls.
He calls us today and every day.

'Thrust out a little from the land.'
Do not be earth bound, or desk bound.

Begin to learn 'the glorious liberty of the children of God'. Move out from the crowd and noise each day, so that you may have a little space around you. So that you may know He is in your boat, your house, your life. If you do not do this, you are hardly ready for the next call, 'Launch out into the deep.' Learn to live in the deep, with a deeper awareness of the world, your neighbour and your God. Of the Celts, Robin Flower wrote:

> It was not only that these scribes and anchorites lived by the destiny of their dedication in an environment of wood and sea; it was because they brought to that environment an eye washed miraculously clear by continuous spiritual exercise that they, first in Europe, had that strange vision of natural things in an almost unnatural purity.[40]

Let us learn to move from the superficial to the deep. Life is not meant to be a perpetual game of trivial pursuits, it is far more glorious than that.

PRAY

'Tis God's will I would do,
My own will I would rein;
Would give to God his due,
From my own due refrain;
God's path I would pursue,
My own path would disdain.[41]

May God shield us by each sheer drop,
May Christ keep us on each rock-path,
May the Spirit fill us on each bare slope,
As we cross hill and plain,
Who live and reign
One God forever. Amen.[42]

Promise that each day you will set apart a little time to discover the depths of things, that you will thrust out a little from the land. Seek to enter the depths of Creation that are all around us, that you may see more clearly. Do not be content with the merely superficial.

Adoration

I bow before the Father
Who made me
I bow before the Son
Who saved me
I bow before the Spirit
Who guides me
In love and adoration
I give my lips
I give my heart
I give my mind
I give my strength
I bow and adore thee
Sacred Three
The Ever One
The Trinity

*Between Weakness
and Strength*

ST LUKE

Come Lord

Come Lord, come light, come love.
Come down,
Come in,
Come among us.
Come Presence, come peace, come power.
Come down,
Come in,
Come among us.
Come Grace, come glory, come goodness.
Come down,
Come in,
Come among us.
Come Creator, come Redeemer, come Strengthener,
Come down,
Come in,
Come among us.
Come Father, come Son, come Spirit,
Come down,
Come in,
Come among us.

Ebb Tide

The ebb tide is the autumn of life, the season that is also called 'the fall'. It is the time when powers begin to wane, abilities recede, we can fall apart, and some talents even fall off. Ebb tide is often the time of nostalgia, when we look back with fondness, for we are not all that comfortable in the present. The ebb tide feeling is expressed well by Wordsworth in his 'Intimations of Immortality',

> There was a time when meadow, grove, and stream,
> The earth, and every common sight,
>   To me did seem
>   Apparelled in celestial light,
> The glory and the freshness of a dream.
> It is not now as it hath been of yore; –
>   Turn wheresoe'er I may,
>   By night or day,
> The things which I have seen I now can see no more.

This is romantic nostalgia. But we may feel it with great agony of spirit. As the tide ebbs we may discover a great emptiness that nothing we do or say can fill. For many this is a time of troubled spirits. This desperate state is captured by Shakespeare in *Hamlet*:

> I have of late – but wherefore I know not – lost all my mirth, forgone all custom of exercise; and indeed it goes so heavily with my disposition that this goodly frame, the earth, seems to me a sterile promontory; this most excellent canopy, the air, look you, this brave o'erhanging firmament, this majestical roof fretted with golden fire, why, it appears no other thing to me but a foul and pestilent congregation of vapours. What a piece of work is man! How noble in reason! how infinite in faculty! in form and moving,

how express and admirable! in action how like an angel! in apprehension how like a god! the beauty of the world! the paragon of animals! And yet, to me, what is this quintessence of dust?[1]

There is hardly a time like the ebb tide for the questioning of life and the feeling that it is quite meaningless. It is a time that is for most quite frightening and threatening. A time when we feel alone and often misunderstood. It is partly because most people are afraid to admit that their life ebbs in any way: we all so badly want to be seen as succeeding and being fulfilled. Yet the truth is, we all must experience ebb tides if we are to know the flow. How we deal with them will depend on our relationship with God. In 1968 the BBC television produced a song for a series called 'Grief and Glory' which reflects how alone many feel at the ebb tide:

> Now the earth has put on cold
> And the stars have turned old,
> And man knows how they were made,
> He has grief and glory inside him,
> And he seeks someone to guide him,
> And sings of love unknown.[2]

But for the Christian, hard though this time is, he still has Glory inside him, he still has Someone to guide him, he still has a love that is known. Even if in this tide awareness ebbs, the reality remains. The Presence is not dependent on our feelings or on our ability. God is in the ebb as much as the flow. So Alistair Maclean can write in *Hebridean Altars*:

As the rain hides the stars, as the autumn mists hide the hills, as the clouds veil the blue of the sky, so the dark happenings of my lot hide the shining of Thy face from me. Yet, if I may hold Thy hand in the darkness, it is enough. Since I know that, though I may stumble in my going, Thou dost not fall.[3]

Again he writes:

> Even though the day be laden and my task dreary and
> my strength small, a song keeps singing in my heart.
> For I know that I am Thine. I am part of Thee. Thou
> art kin to me and all my times are in Thy hand.[4]

This is certainly a time that will put our faith to the
test, whatever we have built on. But it is also a time of
new opportunities, for it is a time of change. We need to
make ourselves aware of what is being revealed on the
shore. Our way of life may of necessity change, but we
carry within ourselves many riches. Just as the ebb
deposits the seaweed on the beaches which it has
brought up from the depths, even so out of our deeps
new things can be revealed.

If we have lived in awareness of God we may, even at
this time, be able to speak boldly, aware that the tide
flows elsewhere and that once again it will come
flooding in our main. We may even speak the last lines
of T. S. Eliot's *Elder Statesman* with confidence in a
loving Father:

> Age and decrepitude can have no terrors for me,
> Loss and vicissitude cannot appal me,
> Not even death can dismay or amaze me
> Fixed in the certainty of love unchanging.
>   I feel utterly secure
> In you; I am a part of you. Now take me to my
>   father.[5]

In the fall we learn of our frailty, that 'the sea is so large
and our boat is so small.' But it can be a time when we
awaken our God within us. A time when we learn that
'God so loved the world that He gave His only begotten
Son that all who believe in Him should not perish, but
have everlasting life.'[6]

Journeying

I set my little ship to sea
Let thine eye Lord be over me
My little craft upon the brine
Keep me Lord for I am thine.

This day dear Lord with me go
If life ebb or if it flow
This day dear Lord be with me
On firm ground or all at sea

    God ahead, God behind
    God be on the path I wind
    God above, God below
    God be everywhere I go
    God in the steep
    God in the shade
    God me safe keep
    Come to my aid.

Sea Tides

Let the love tide swelling
Surround me and my dwelling.
Let the power of the mighty sea
Flow in, Lord, and strengthen me,
Tide of Christ covering my shore
That I may live for evermore.

Whatever the tide
The Lord at my side,
In storm or in calm
To keep me from harm,
In good or in ill
He's with me still.

Some things in life ebb as others flow,
and some things flow as others ebb.
Lord, let my praises never reach an ebb tide.

Presence

Be with us Lord
To find your hopefulness.

Be with us Lord
In the land beyond all stress.

Be with us Lord
To give us your deep peace.

Be with us Lord
At life's final release.

Be with us Lord
Now and in our final hour.

Be with us Lord
And fill us with your power.

Have Mercy

Lord of space
Lord of time
Lord of life
            Have mercy.

God of sun
God of stars
God of earth
            Have mercy.

Jesus of Mary
Jesus of Nazareth
Jesus of Gethsemane
            Have mercy.

Christ of cross
Christ of tomb
Christ risen
            Have mercy.

Spirit on high
Spirit nearby
Spirit of calm
            Have mercy.

Spirit of grace
Spirit of talents
Spirit of life
            Have mercy.

Kyries

Lord have mercy
>> On your creation,
>> On the world you have made,
>> On every living creature,
>> On me.
>>> Lord have mercy

Christ have mercy
>> On your salvation,
>> On those who are lost,
>> On those who stray,
>> On me.
>>> Christ have mercy

Lord have mercy
>> On the de-spirited,
>> On the depressed,
>> On the despairing,
>> On me.
>>> Lord have mercy

And With Your Spirit

The Lord be with you.
And with your spirit too.

Today, tonight,
In shade and light,
The Lord be with you.
And with your spirit too.

In weakness and pain,
In powers that wane,
The Lord be with you.
And with your spirit too.

In health and in might,
In strength for the fight,
The Lord be with you.
And with your spirit too.

In your coming to rest,
In rising with the blessed,
The Lord be with you.
And with your spirit too.

Desert Waters

O spring in the desert
O shelter from the heat
O light in the darkness
O guide for the feet
O joy in our sadness
O support for the weak
O Lord with us always
Your Presence we seek.

128

Strength through Faith

I arise today
Through a mighty strength, the invocation of the
  Trinity.

Life had been getting increasingly hard, so I ran away.
For a while at least, I would escape; I went into the
Cheviot Hills. The morning was spent winding down,
watching the dipper on the River Breamish and a
buzzard circling on the air currents. The afternoon was
filled with the sound of the cuckoo. Suddenly the valley
darkened; it was only a cloud, but all my troubles
returned with it. The beauties of the valley were still
there, but I could no longer see them or hear them; I
was distracted, out of tune. Perhaps if I climbed the hill
tops I would see the sun again.

In a while I reached the summit, climbing over a
great heap of stones into a Bronze Age fortress. I sat in
this great circle of stones to get my breath back, and
looked out towards the North Sea in the direction of
Holy Island. A great storm was brewing and coming my
way. I watched the louring clouds racing towards the
hills, yet they never came. The hills seemed to break the
clouds and divide them: the storm went to the north and
south, but it did not come over me. In that ancient circle
built to protect ancient man, I suddenly felt protected. I
was surrounded by the Presence and Power of God. He
would not leave me or forsake; I could not slip out of
His love or care. The words of a hymn came to mind,
and I spoke them as an act of faith:

> The storm may roar without me,
> My heart may low be laid,
> But God is round about me
> And can I be dismayed?

The Presence of God is an eternal fact. He never leaves us alone or forsakes us. It is when we lose sight of Him that we falter and sink beneath the waves. We need to regain a clear vision of the Presence, to perceive the reality of His relationship with us and act upon it.

Not long ago, I was in a little grey chapel in a valley. The preacher was rather tedious and the hymns dull. I could have endured both, but when he started his prayers by saying, 'Now I just want you to imagine God is present,' I could have wept. I now knew why it was such heavy going: he did not know of the Presence, he could only imagine it. God is beyond our greatest imagination; either He is present, and that influences everything we do, or He is absent, and then we are poor indeed.

Faith is the discovery that He is at hand: 'in Him we live and move and have our being.' Faith is the joy of knowing that we dwell in Him and He in us. You cannot imagine this, you cannot even make it happen, but you can experience it as a fact. It is necessary to keep ourselves sensitive, what the Celt calls 'to tune the five-stringed harp', to keep each of our five senses alert to the fact of God and His surrounding Presence. There, in the Cheviot Hills, I became in tune once more. For a while I had lost sight of the beauty of the earth; no wonder I was blind to the glories of the Presence. Now all came back to me as I opened myself to them. I made an affirmation of my faith to the God who is about me and said aloud:

> Circle me O God
> Keep hope within
> Despair without.
>
> Circle me O God
> Keep peace within
> Keep turmoil out.

Circle me O God
Keep calm within
Keep storms without.

Circle me O God
Keep strength within
Keep weakness out.

Here I rediscovered a power and a strength that was not my own: I turned to God who knows that we have no power of ourselves. I had discovered what the Celtic people call the *Caim*, the Encircling.

It is said that when the Celtic saints were troubled by evil or attacked by enemies, they drew the *Caim* around them. Sometimes they actually made a circle around themselves by using a stick or their index finger. This was no magic, but an expression of the reality of the Presence of God. The encompassing of any of the Three Persons of the Trinity, or all of them, might be called on. In old times the suppliant would stretch out the right hand with the index finger extended, while turning around sunwise, as if on a pivot, and calling for the desired Presence to protect him. The circle was said to accompany the person on his journey and keep him from dangers.

This was a way of acting out the truth stated by Paul in Romans:

If God is for us, who can be against us? . . .
I am certain that nothing can separate us from his
    love: neither death nor life,
neither angels nor other heavenly rulers or
    powers,
neither the present nor the future,
neither the world above or the world below –
    there is nothing in all creation that will ever be
    able to separate us from the love of God
    which is ours through Christ Jesus our Lord.[7]

Once this becomes our own personal experience, life becomes quite different. The *Caim* works, not as a charm, but to re-tune us to the reality of the love and presence of God. I like to listen to my transistor in the morning to hear the news. When I first come into the room all is silent, the radio waves are there, but I have not switched on; the transistor does not create the music, it only receives it. I need to switch on and be tuned in. So it is with the Divine Presence. By calling upon Him, we tune ourselves to His being with us.

The Hymn of St Patrick is used like a *Caim*:

> *I arise today*
> *Through a mighty strength, the invocation*
> *Of the Trinity.*

Call upon the Father; take your time. You may like to see yourself as if a child with a heavy load to carry. You have been struggling with this, feeling that it will defeat you; it is too heavy for you, it is wearing you out. The Father is there. Call upon Him. He has been watching and waiting. He will not only help you to carry your load; He will carry you if you are weary. Call upon Him. Let His arms enfold you, His love surround you.

> The encircling God is with you,
> The encircling Power of the Creator.

Call upon the Saviour. It is when we are unable to help ourselves that we begin to know Christ as our Saviour. Call upon Him who has conquered death and all the hells of this world. With His wounded hands He will enfold you. He calls you: 'Come to me all of you who are tired from carrying heavy loads, and I will give you rest.'[8] Come, trust in Him.

> The enfolding of Christ be round you,
> The enfolding arms of His love.

Come to the Lord and giver of Life. Come to the Spirit, who transforms you from a 'lump of clay' to a living being, a person. Come to the Spirit to be refreshed, renewed, restored.

The encompassing of the Spirit be round you,
The encompassing of the strength of God.

This is how to begin the day, not in your own effort, but in the power of God. Awake to this fact and it will help you to arise – not only to get up, but to get over so many things that would pull you down. The way to overcome gravity – and so much triviality – is to arise in the Presence each morning. To know that we are the sons and daughters of God, that He is with us and that He gives us life eternal. He gives today a resurrection quality, and helps us to *arise*. St Paul says of this:

We who have this spiritual treasure are like common clay pots, in order to show that the supreme power belongs to God, not us. We are often troubled, but not crushed; sometimes in doubt, but never in despair; there are many enemies, but we are never without a friend; and though badly hurt at times, we are not destroyed.[9]

Because such prayers are like pulling a coat around us when the weather becomes severe, many of them became dressing prayers. They were like St Paul putting on 'the whole armour of God'. In her translation of the St Patrick's Breastplate, Mrs Alexander makes it sound as if Patrick is fastening the Presence to himself: binding God to him as carefully as he binds on his shoes or his tunic. Perhaps as he was dressing he would say:

I bind unto myself today
The strong name of the Trinity,
By invocation of the same,
The Three in One and One in Three.

As he threads the laces through the eye-holes of his tunic and pulls them tight about his body, he continues:

> *I bind this day to me for ever,*
> *By power of faith, Christ's Incarnation;*
> *His baptism in the Jordan River;*
> *His death on cross for my salvation.*

This is not a God of the remote past, a historical God, nor is it a God of the distant future, but a God who is near at hand ready to help. He is our God *today*. It is today that we are able to meet Him.

Sometimes such prayer has been compared with the modern idea of positive thinking, but it is far more than that. Positive thinking is dangerously near to suggesting that we are self-sufficient, that it is all in the mind and we are always able to help ourselves. Life in the end must always prove this to be a lie. The *Caim* and dressing prayers are putting our trust in a power beyond ourselves. Positive thinking tends to be egocentric; our prayers are God-centred, discovering that we are centred in God, without whom nothing is strong.

David Gascoyne expresses it so well:

Always, whenever, whatever, however,
When I am able to resist
For once the constant pressure of failure to exist
Let me remember
That to be truly man is to be man aware of thee
And unfraid to be. So help me God.[10]

EXERCISES

1. *Pause in the Presence*. 'In the beginning God'. This is how the Bible begins, and this is how prayer must begin. Words without the Presence remain just words, but we are not without the Presence. Let the Word become flesh and dwell among us that we may hold His glory.

In the Beginning GOD

In the beginning of space
          of time
          of the universe, GOD.

In the beginning of creation
          of life
          of mankind, GOD.

In the beginning of individuals
          of personalities
          of me, GOD.

In the beginning of this year
          of this week
          of this hour, GOD.

In the beginning of each thought
          of each word
          of each deed, GOD.

Add to this any beginnings you feel are important to you this day. Know that He abides with you and surrounds you.

'As He was in the beginning, He is now and shall be forever, God.' Amen.

2. *Practise the Caim*. Know that we dwell in Him and He in us.

        Your Presence is in my life
        Your Presence is all around me
        Your Presence is Peace.

        Your Presence is in my house
        Your Presence is all around me
        Your Presence is Peace.

Your Presence is in my work
Your Presence is all around me
Your Presence is Peace.

Choose new statements in the first line to express where you need to affirm His Presence. Make them really personal; your Presence is in the tube (underground), on the bus, in the factory . . .

Change the last word of the last line. Substitute whatever gift of the Presence you seek – 'your Presence is love . . . joy . . . strength . . . healing . . . restoring.' But do use the same phrase often: not to make it happen, but to know it is already true.

You may like to make a circle when you begin, knowing that God does encircle you. Like a ripple caused by a stone on a pond, you may like to ever increase your circle. Start with yourself, your home, your street, and move ever outward. Picture each in turn surrounded also by the Love, Peace and Presence of God.

3. PAUSE, PRESENCE, PICTURE, PONDER, PROMISE

PAUSE   Stop what you are doing. Let yourself relax; let all the tension go out of your body, all troubled thoughts out of your mind . . . Make space in your life for something to happen . . . Make room for God.
Let go, and let God.
Breathe slowly and deeply . . .
Be still . . .

PRESENCE   . . . know that God is with you.
This is the purpose of this exercise – to discover that God is with you.
'God unseen yet ever near
Thy Presence may I feel.'
The Presence is to be enjoyed.
Let God take over . . . Do not try to do

anything at this stage but to be aware of Him and rest in His Presence. Make little acts of affirmation.

'Lord you are here. Help me to know it.'

'Lord you are love. Help me to receive you.'

PICTURE what this fact of Presence means for you today. Your God is with you: you dwell in Him and He in you. He is with you at work, at rest, at play.

PONDER Think what this should mean for each of those situations.

We are never alone. There is an abiding Presence; strength, love, peace, forgiveness are ever at hand. 'My Presence will go with you and I will give you rest.'

PROMISE to recall the fact of His Presence throughout the day, perhaps by using the *Caim*. Promise:

'I will arise today,
Through a mighty strength, the invocation of the
*   Trinity.'*

My Fortress

God is my fortress
God is my might
God is my Saviour
God is my right
God is my helper
All the day long
God is the Power
Making me strong.

The Conqueror

Lord strengthen every good
Defeat the power of evil

Lord strengthen every light
Defeat the power of darkness

Lord strengthen every power
Defeat the power of weakness

Lord strengthen every joy
Defeat the power of sadness

Lord strengthen every love
Defeat the power of hatred

Lord strengthen every life
Defeat the power of death

Redeemer

Come Lord and save
                Your creation from evil,
                Your world from corruption,
                Your earth from oppression.

Come Lord and save
                Your children from captivity,
                Your people from injustice,
                Your image from darkness.

Come Lord and save
                Your church from error,
                Your chosen from pride,
                Your Body from dis-ease.

Come Lord and save
                Your loved one from weakness,
                Your dear one from wasting,
                Your redeemed one from death.

Thou Art God

Thou art the peace of all things calm
Thou art the place to hide from harm
Thou art the light that shines in dark
Thou art the heart's eternal spark
Thou art the door that's open wide
Thou art the guest who waits inside
Thou art the stranger at the door
Thou art the calling of the poor
Thou art my Lord and with me still
Thou art my love, keep me from ill
Thou art the light, the truth, the way
Thou art my Saviour this very day.

Be thou my great Father, and I thy true son;
be thou in me dwelling, and I with thee one.

I watched a young lad and his father prepare to climb a rock face with a slight overhang. The boy was very young, perhaps even a little frightened, but very excited that they would ascend. The father was big and strong and obviously experienced. Before beginning the climb, the father reminded his son of the dangers and the need for caution. There would times when the son could not see him, but he assured the lad that he would be there. More than this, before they proceeded, the father bound them together by a rope and shackles. 'Now if you get into difficulties, I will be there and able to help you. Don't be afraid, you know how strong I am. I will not let you fall. Even in the worst bits, when you cannot see me, know we are joined together, you just need to give tug on the rope and I will respond. Don't worry about anything; I am there all the time, I won't let anything hurt you.' I watched them set off on this great adventure. The father knew the way and could have scaled it quite quickly but he set his pace to that of his son. The father led the way and they both began to ascend. I could see the confidence the father gave the son. I could see the father on the rock face even when the son could not. I watched them until they reached the top. What a wonderful relationship. What a wealth of images this event gave me.

It is good when we know that our safety and well-being are not dependent on our own strength, our own cleverness or even our own virtue. Our Father cares, and our well-being and safety are dependent on His presence and His love. It is of primary importance that

143

we experience that loving relationship with God that is expressed in the word 'Father'. What matters is that we come to know for ourselves that He cares, He comes to us, He dwells with us and that He is 'mindful of us'. No matter what we have done or where we have wandered, He will welcome us home. It is He who will provide us with support and a new confidence. It is such a shame for us if we have lost sight of this, for then the darkness really threatens and there is no provision in the storms except our own feeble fantasies.

The age in which we live is hardly one of assurance or of awareness of the Presence. More than once, the modern person has been likened to an orphan on a lost planet. People genuinely feel alone in a hostile environment and with very little to guide them. In the twentieth century it seems that so many have lost any vital relationship with the Father. This is all the more reason for us to hold on to the reality of God as our Father. We must not let the images of the Fatherhood of God be lost through the confusion of the present age.

In his novel *The Castle*, Kafka portrays the loneliness and the confusion of our times. The main character, the surveyor, enters the scene without any relations or friends; he has no pedigree and no history, there is no story about his life up to this point. All he has is a letter of appointment as a land surveyor. The place he comes to is a small country town, with its shops, inns and streets. But like many of our newer estates there is no centre to it: the place lacks a heart. It would seem that there is no one who is really in control and no one who particularly wants to be responsive. There is a feeling that all have been dis-spirited. There is, for this reason, a difficulty about relationships – as a child of God, I am aware that when the relationship with the Father is broken, all relationships become more tenuous.

Over this situation broods the castle. You can feel that

the castle is there, that it is important and yet in some ways never quite approachable. This sort of feeling about community and about any God-like figure is very common today. Many have learned to survive without recourse to that 'hypothesis God', but they have hardly learned to live, and relationships seem to break down so easily. There is something about the fullness of life and the fullness of joy that eludes the times in which we live. So many of the communities in which we dwell are like that in Kafka's *Castle*. It feels like a place of famine and of impoverished relationships, and we know in our hearts that it ought to be better. We know that there is a richer way of living.

Jesus talked of such a situation in his story about the Prodigal Son (Luke 15). In seeking to become a possessor in his own right, the prodigal broke his relationship with the father. It was not that the father would not give, it was not that the father moved away. It was the son who was dis-eased; he was not at home in the present, he wanted to own things rather than to have this relationship. The son wanted to make himself the centre of his world. He had come of age and did not need a father. He was to learn by experience that because this relationship is broken, all other relationships break down also.

Francis Thompson expressed this alienation in 'The Hound of Heaven', a poem about man on the run from God. Here are some verse endings. The Pursuer tells the pursued:

'All things betray thee, who betrayest Me.'

'Naught shelters thee, who wilt not shelter Me.'

'Lo! Naught contents thee, who content'st not Me.'

and the final lines:

'Ah, fondest, blindest, weakest,
I am He Whom thou seekest!
Thou dravest love from thee, who dravest Me.'

The prodigal learned that you cannot buy love, it must be freely given or it is less than the genuine article. Soon his bought friends disappear. The richness of relationships gone, the son discovers the emptiness that is within, an emptiness that the land around him cannot satisfy. It is no use possessing things if you are empty inside. This is what Jesus implied when he said, 'What does it profit a man to gain the whole world if he lose his own soul.' Without the knowledge of being loved, life becomes bestial. To share pigs' food is about as low as the prodigal can be without dying. Yet within himself he knows the richness of home. He who was once sick of home carries within himself a homesickness, and nothing will satisfy him until he is home. We must note that his feelings are now about his father's house; his desire and prayer are not for forgiveness but for the father, not to receive something but to relate to someone. The longing is not so much to possess as to be possessed, to be loved. What he seeks is not the restoration of status but the restoration of a relationship. In his heart of hearts, he knows the generosity of the father. The other son would also have to learn that this love cannot be earned, or bought by being law-abiding, it is a gift that is freely given. This relationship is not gained by duty or worked for, it is of the heart, and can only be worked at. Love awakens reciprocal love. Relationships must be two-way in their workings.

Be thou my great Father, and I thy true son . . .
Great Heart of my own heart, whatever befall,
still be thou my vision, thou Ruler of all.

Vision is experienced as a homecoming; we see in depth the place we live in as we have never seen it before. In the Presence of the Father we have a new experience of love, of creation and of our own being. Like Moses, we discover that the place on which we stand is holy ground. Even though we may find ourselves far from home, and in a desert place, when we experience the Presence, we experience a homecoming. Fatherhood is about His availability to us. If we are willing to repent, to turn around, He is already there waiting to receive us. In love He waits for us to come: He has always been 'more ready to hear than we to pray'. He will travel the road with us, offering us His rest. Again and again the prayers of the western Highlands tell of the God who travels with us, of a Father who knows our needs and is ever ready to protect us.

> Thou King of moon and of the sun,
> Of the stars thou lov'd and fragrant King,
> Thou thyself knowest our needs each one,
> O merciful God of everything.
>
> Each day that our moving steps we take,
> Each hour of wakening that we know,
> The dark distress and sorrow we make,
> To the King of hosts who loved us so;
>
> Be with us through the time of each day,
> Be with us through the time of each night,
> Be with us ever each night and day,
> Be with us ever each day and night.[11]

Fatherhood tells us that God is not a god without feelings. He is not a god who made His world and then left it. He is at home in it and cares for it. God loves the world. In fact God so loves the world that He is willing to give Himself for it (see John 3.16). We must not narrow this love just to human beings. God's love is for the whole world and it is the whole world that waits in groaning for His redeeming love.[12] It is such a pity that so many Christians give the impression that we should not love the world. They portray God as a spoil-sport rather than a father. It is not just we that are His – 'The earth is the Lord's and all that therein is: the compass of the world, and they that dwell therein.'[13] One of the prerequisites of vision is that we love the world, and with some fervour and intensity. Love must always involve passion. In his book *Wordsworth and the Artist's Vision* Alec King wrote:

> What is necessary first for visionary power is an undaunted appetite for liveliness – to be among the active elements of the world and to love what they do to you, to love to 'work and to be wrought upon': to be 'alive to all that is enjoyed and all that is endured', to have the loneliness and courage to take in not only joy but dismay and fear and pain as modes of being without bolting for comfort or obscuring them with social chatter.[14]

To experience that the whole world belongs to God and that it is the Father's house, opens up a whole world of discovery. We discover that we are part of something far greater than we ever imagined: we may even begin to comprehend what St Paul meant when he said, 'to those who love God all things work for the good.'[15] All things work together. In God there is no division; in God there is an underlying unity. This is a unity that our world of broken relationships and the fractured universe need to rediscover. We can even discover this unity through looking at ourselves. God has used all of time, all of the world, to create us as individuals. We are linked by fine threads to everything else in the world. The relationship with creation, which we broke in our wandering, is restored when we come home to the

Father. We can then delight to know that God has made us from the minerals of the earth, and recreates us through the plants, the animals and the very air we breathe. We can begin to feel with St Francis that we are genuinely related to Brother Sun and Sister Moon. When we discover this, we learn that God has used these things to make us sons and daughters of God, and that He still uses these things to sustain us. 'St Patrick's Breastplate' expresses this in the verse

> I bind unto myself today
> The virtues of the starlit heaven,
> The glorious sun's life-giving ray,
> The whiteness of the moon at even,
> The flashing of the lightning free,
> The whirling wind's tempestuous shocks,
> The stable earth, the deep salt sea,
> Around the old eternal rocks.

Many of our problems about the greening of the earth, and ecology, have been created through our own insensitivity. We have lost sight of our roots and of our relatedness to all things. Nothing stands completely alone in this world, all things affect other things that are around them. If we have lost a love for creation, we cannot say we love its Creator. If we do not show respect for what the Father has in His house, we should not be surprised that we are not at home in His Presence, or in His world. Learn that God touches you through all of creation, that He offers himself to you through His world. He is truly incarnate in His world. In his 'Mass on the World', Teilhard de Chardin says it is the purpose of life to discover the union between God and his universe:

> For me, my God, all joy and all achievement, the very purpose of my being and all my love of life, all

depend on this one basic vision of the union between yourself and the universe. Let others, fulfilling a function more august than mine, proclaim your splendours as pure Spirit; as for me, dominated as I am by a vocation which springs from the inmost fibres of my being, I have no desire, I have no ability, to proclaim anything except the innumerable pro- longations of your incarnate Being in the world of matter: I can preach only the mystery of your flesh, you the Soul shining forth through all that surrounds us.[16]

If the Father makes Himself at home in the world, so must we. At this stage of our life this is the only world we have got; if we do not appreciate it, then it is hardly proper to expect the Creator of it to offer us another at any time.

Fatherhood also expresses a personal care for each of us. We are His sons and daughters and He knows our needs. He is concerned about our provisions, about our daily bread. When it comes to food and clothing, our heavenly Father knows that we have need of such things. The God who clothes the grass and feeds the birds of the air, provides for us His sons and daughters. This love of the Father, though it is directed to the whole world, is deeply individual. He cares for each son and daughter individually. He calls each of us by name. 'The Lord said to Moses, I will do this thing also that thou hast spoken: for thou hast found grace in my sight, and I know thee by name.'[17] Or in Isaiah: 'I will give thee the treasures of darkness, and hidden riches of secret places, that thou mayest know that I, the Lord, which call thee by thy name, am the God of Israel.'[18]

There was a time when I tired easily of all those lists of names that you find in the Bible, I was not all that interested in who begat who. Now I know that every name is important; without that link in the chain the rest could not have happened. Someone may have seemed insignificant in their time, but without them the world would not be the same. You just have to look at the lineage of Jesus to understand that. Who would have thought that from some of those doubtful characters God Himself would come forth? God is interested in us individually.

As our Father, He has a personal interest in us:

> For only a penny you can buy two sparrows, yet not one sparrow falls to the ground without your Father's consent. As for you, even the hairs of your head have all been counted. So do not be afraid; you are worth much more than many sparrows![19]

This love, this Presence, this indwelling, is waiting for us to turn to Him, that He may fill our lives with goodness and peace. All that is asked of us is that we come to our senses, that we become truly aware that we are sons and daughters of God, that He is a personal God and seeks a personal relationship with us. Because this relationship is a living one, it is not static. It is a relationship that will grow, a relationship in which we are increasing more and more.

> He was in the world, and the world was made by him, and the world knew him not. He came unto his own, and his own received him not. But as many as received him, to them gave he power to become the sons of God . . . God himself was their Father.[20]

To return to the Presence is to enter into a new harmony with the world and to discover an inner peace. This peace is one that the world cannot give and that the world cannot take from us. It is personal, God dwelling in us and we in God. We will have a new assurance in the dark and a new hope for the future. We can express it like this:

I am serene because I know that thou lovest me.
Because thou lovest me, naught can move me from
my peace.
Because thou lovest me, I am one to whom all good
has come.[21]

I do not think that I shall fear thee when I see thee
face to face. For I call to mind my father, he who was
the true man and the kind. And my mother, the pure
one, out of whose heart flowed the waters of healing.
And, as I think of them, my pulses beat with joy and
cry to thee, Father, and say: 'Thou art more and
tenderer than they.' Therefore when I am come into
the court of thy presence I know that thou wilt look
upon me with my father's eyes and with my mother's
pity and thou wilt draw me to thy breast.[22]

Be thou my great Father, and I thy true son;
be thou in me dwelling, and I with thee one.

EXERCISES

1. Use the story of the Prodigal Son as a theme for meditation.

PAUSE
Stop all that you are doing.
Are you aware of where you are? Spend a little time just
opening up in awareness to what is around you.
Do you hear Him who calls you by name, who wants to
know you personally?
Are you responding to His love?
Be still now in His Presence, and let Him enfold you in His
love.

PRESENCE
Explore a little the fact that you are in His Presence.
Be aware that He is offering Himself to you.
Open your life to Him.

Do not talk about Him, talk to Him.
Enjoy giving yourself to Him as He gives Himself to you.
Say quietly: You, Lord, are in this Place.
   Your Presence fills it.
   Your Presence is Love.

PICTURE
See yourself as the prodigal son or daughter.
Using your senses, imagine you leave home,
taking with you everything you possibly can.
Do you see the tears in your Father's eyes?
Are you aware of the pain in His heart?
You never turn back – He watches until you are out of
 sight.
Picture the good time, and the things you buy – including
 friends.
But it does not last. Picture similar events in your life.
Now experience the hunger, shame, loneliness.
See yourself in the pigsty – know that you are far from
 home.
Look back with longing to the happier times.
Turn around, seek to return, make your way home.
Long before home is in sight, He is there.
He has been longing for you, searching for you.
He runs to meet you with open arms.
He asks for no explanations.
He enfolds you in His love.

PONDER
Are you sure you have come Home and are not just after
 bed and breakfast? Think upon these words of St
 Augustine:

  He who seeks from God
  Anything less than God
  Esteems the gifts of God
  More than the giver.

Have you really come to Him, or are you just looking for a
 safe haven?
Do you want to be possessed more than to possess?
After having made the journey and been accepted – are
 you still staying outside? Though you are welcome, are
 you still at heart in a far country?

That you will seek to draw near to God – and let Him draw near to you.

2. Consider and visualise these words of Mother Julian:

He is our clothing, for love; He enwraps us and envelops us, embraces us and encloses us; He hovers over us, for tender love, that He may never leave us . . .

In this He shewed me a little thing, the quantity of a hazel nut, lying in the palm of my hand, and to my understanding it was as round as any ball. I looked thereupon and thought: 'What may this be?' And I was answered in a general way thus: 'It is all that is made.' I marvelled how it could last, for methought it might fall suddenly to naught for littleness. And I was answered in my understanding: 'It lasts and ever shall last because God loves it, and so hath all-thing its being through the love of God.'

In this little thing I saw three parts. The first is God made it; the second is that He loves it; the third that He keeps it. But what is that to me? Insooth, the Maker, the Lover, the Keeper.[23]

Now choose some material object that tells you that He is its Maker, Lover, and Keeper.

Finally apply each of these words to yourself. Visualise what is implied when you accept that God is your Maker, Lover, and Keeper.

3. Grant us, O Lord, to awake out of sleep,
   out of unbelief, little belief, dull belief,
   out of death, into faith;
   and by hearing thy word,
           obeying thy will,
           doing thy works,
   to pass from darkness to light,
           from ignorance to knowledge,
           from blindness to sight;

to move from repentance to pardon,
  from allegiance to love,
  from lethargy to power:
And so, declare thee, Father,
  and thee, Redeemer Lord,
  and the holy and life-giving Spirit,
  one God, almighty, all loving,
  world without end.[24]

  Be thou my great Father, and I thy true son;
  be thou in me dwelling and I with thee one.

In the Father's power
In the Son's power
In the Spirit's power
Be this hour

Father be my friend
Jesus be my friend
Spirit be my friend
To the journey's end

Father be my guard
Jesus be my guard
Spirit be my guard
When the way is hard

In the Father's power
In the Son's power
In the Spirit's power
Be this hour

Grace

Lord you are

         Grace for our needs
         Strength for our weakness
         Light for our blindness
         Love for our loneliness
         Word for our deafness
         Joy for our weariness
         Peace for our anxiousness
         Wonder for our dullness
         Saviour for our hopelessness

Lord you are

         Grace for our needs.

Powerful Hand

O powerful hand grant (me)
Your might.
O guiding hand grant (me)
Your light.
O healing hand grant (me)
Your balm.
O saving hand grant (me)
Your calm.
O loving hand grant (me)
Your peace.
O redeeming hand grant (me)
Your release.

Affirmations

I believe O God of all gods that you are
The Eternal Father of Life

I believe O God of all gods that you are
The Eternal Father of Love

I believe O God of all gods that you are
The Eternal Father of Peace

I believe O God of all gods that you are
The Eternal Father of Joy

I believe O God of all gods that you are
The Eternal Father of the saints

I believe O God of all gods that you are
The Eternal Father the Creator

I believe O God of all gods that you are
The Eternal Father strong to save

I believe O God of all gods that you are
The Eternal Father of me.

Come Holy Dove

When I feel alone
Your Presence is ever with me.
Come Holy Dove
Cover with love.

When I am in the dark
Your light is all around me.
Come Holy Dove
Cover with love.

When I am in the cold
Your warmth will enfold me.
Come Holy Dove
Cover with love.

When I feel weak
Your strength will seek me.
Come Holy Dove
Cover with love.

When I am sad
Your joy will make me glad.
Come Holy Dove
Cover with love.

When I am sick and ill
Your health will heal me still.
Come Holy Dove
Cover with love.

Spirit be about my head
Spirit peace around me shed
Spirit light about my way
Spirit guardian night and day

Come Holy Dove
Cover with love

In This Frail Craft

PAUSE

In the Presence of God. Know that you are never alone, that He is always with you. Stop your busy-ness and your struggles to know that He is there. Hear Him say, 'Be still, and know that I am God.' Perhaps you have never really called on Him before: stop all that you are doing, even reading this, and do so now. Know that we cannot survive this life alone, and call upon Him. Take time to realise that amidst the storms of life He is with you. He never leaves you. Relax, knowing He is there. No need for effort to bring Him. Just call upon Him and awaken Him.

You are with Him in this place where you are, and He is with you. Say:

> You, Lord, are in my life
> Your Presence fills it
> Your Presence is Peace.
>
> You Lord are in the Storm
> Your Presence fills it
> Your Presence is Peace.

Know that in this frail craft which we call 'life', He is present.

PICTURE

Picture the disciples in their boat. The day started off well: there were crowds of people clamouring to see Jesus, bringing their troubles for His healing, their anxieties for His calming. The sky was blue and the water like a mill pond. Everything in the world seemed lovely. A good day to be alive. They move away from the crowds and on to the sea. They are tired after a busy day, everyone wants a rest. The gentle rocking of the boat and the lapping of the waters soon have them all resting. Jesus is now asleep in the boat.

What happens next takes them all by surprise, even the seasoned fishermen. A storm hits the boat. Great winds have come from nowhere. The waves rise and dark clouds lower. At first it is just spray that prevents them from seeing clearly, then great waves beat against and enter their boat. They are being driven further and further from the shore and from the area that they know well. They are alone and so small, the sea so large. They are so frail, the waves so mighty and strong. Soon they will be overwhelmed: soon they will perish. Meanwhile, Jesus sleeps in the boat.

Yes, Jesus is there. He has not saved them from the storm. He is there with them in the storm and this will not be the last time. He is there to be called upon. There to be awakened. Yet the disciples try everything they can – to no avail. Soon, it seems, human frailty will be swamped – so they cry out, 'Lord save us, we are perishing!' It will not be the last time they feel like this. The storm is raging about them, they and their vessel are so fragile. Jesus then awakens. He stands amidst the wind and waves, He is there in the storms of life, and He says, 'Peace, be still,' He stills the noise of the waves, the raging of the wind, and the mounting fears of the disciples. They may be now entering a strange country, but they have a new-found peace; for a little while all around them is calm. They are still learning that 'God so loved the world that He gave his only begotten Son, that we should not perish, but have everlasting life.'

PONDER

Think about these words of Julian of Norwich:

> He did not say, 'You shall not be tempest-tossed,
> you shall not be weary,
> you shall not be discomforted.'
> But He said, 'You shall not be overcome.'

Once we believe in Jesus, we do not escape the storms and troubles of life. In fact, in some strange sense more storms than ever seem to come our way. Perhaps we should expect this. If there is any power of evil in the world, we should expect it to oppose anything or anyone that is trying to do what is right and good. However, all of us will meet with storms; there will be times when the tide ebbs on us and we know our human frailty. For all of us will come the experience that we are 'perishing', no matter how far we try and run from it or hide. But for all this God loves and God cares. And there is more. He has sent His Son that we should not perish. In this frail craft that we call life He is present, just waiting to be awakened. Let us learn to call upon Him. Our lives are often like a little boat on a great and stormy sea. It is expressed well by the Hebridean saying;

> So frail our boat, so great yon sea.

Know that we are never left alone, and He does not want us to be overcome.

PRAY

Here is a prayer thought from the Hebrides:

> Round our skiff be God's aboutness
> Ere she try the deeps of sea,
> Sea-shell frail for all her stoutness
> Unless Thou her Helmsman be.[26]

The following prayer could have been known by the early Celts. It is by St Augustine:

Blessed are all your saints, O God and King, who have travelled over the tempestuous sea of this life and have made the harbour of peace and felicity. Watch over us who are still on this dangerous voyage. Frail is our vessel, and the ocean wide: but as in your mercy you have set our course, so pilot the vessel of our life towards the everlasting shore of peace, and bring us at last to the quiet haven of our heart's desire; through Jesus Christ our Lord. Amen.

PROMISE

To call upon the Presence regularly, especially when powers ebb or storms increase. Learn to say regularly:

Lord, save us, we are perishing.

Until the Tide Turns

Lord,
I wait for the tide to turn
Until the distant becomes close,
Until the far off becomes near,
Until the outside is within,
Until the ebb flows.

Lord,
I wait for the tide to turn
Until weakness is made strong,
Until blindness turns to sight,
Until the fractured is made whole,
Until the ebb flows.

Lord,
I wait until the tide turns,
Until the ordinary becomes strange,
Until the empty is Presence-full,
Until the two become one,
Until the ebb flows.

*Between Dying
and Living*

ST JOHN

Come, Creator

From chaos and emptiness,
From loneliness and lifelessness,
              Come, Creator, Come.

From darkness and shapelessness,
From the abyss and awfulness,
              Come, Creator, Come

From fearfulness and hopelessness,
From weakness and dreadfulness,
              Come, Creator, Come.

Death is Not Fatal

I arise today
Through the strength of his crucifixion with his
*   burial.*

Celtic and Anglo-Saxon stone crosses are full of symbolism and fascination. A favourite of mine is the cross at Stonegrave Minster near Helmsley in North Yorkshire. The shaft of the cross is covered with a typical interlacing in a criss-cross pattern: this represents life – it looks simple, but in fact is very complex. As the line travels over the whole of the shaft, it goes over and under, under and over itself, just as life has its ups and downs: sometimes you are on top of the world and at other times things get you down. If you follow this line, it is usually endless. For the Christian, that is a strong statement about life.

The criss-cross pattern also represents the weaving of life by the fates: the fact that our life is limited, our freedoms restricted. Like the stonemason, we are only able to work within fixed parameters. So much is already laid out, measured for us. Some would argue that we are in the hands of fate, predestined from the start. But the pattern is not allowed to take over. Fate does not have the last word. It is not the final explanation of life. Superimposed, bedded right into the pattern, are three figures. There is a majestically powerful figure at the top, holding up the pillars of the world. He is above all and has command. He looks like Atlas with the world, the wheeled cross-head, on his shoulders. He upholds us at all times.

At the base of the cross is a squared figure of a man holding a book. Often Celtic missionaries are shown with a book-satchel around their neck. Here is our guide and strengthener, the Spirit of God.

171

Central to the shaft is an empty cross, without the pattern of the fates. It is the sign of Jesus triumphant, neither the cross nor the grave could keep Him. He is let loose in the world. The message is that we are not in the hands of fate, but in the hands of the Almighty; death is not fatal.

In John 11.4, where Jesus is trying to explain to the disciples about Lazarus, He says: 'The final result of this illness will not be the death of Lazarus . . . and it will be the means by which the Son of God will receive glory.' Jesus is trying to tell them that death is not the end, not a terminal disease; but it is hard to understand. In verse 11 of the same chapter, Jesus says: 'Our friend Lazarus has fallen asleep, but I will go and wake him up.' The disciples still find it difficult to comprehend, so Jesus says plainly, 'Lazarus is dead.' Still, He had promised to come and awaken him, and that He did. The Celtic Church was very much in the tradition of St John's Gospel – believing that death is a grave matter, but not fatal!

It is because Christians believe that death is not the end that they dare risk their lives and even court martyrdom. By their death, the martyrs witnessed fully to their faith in eternal life; death is but the gate to glory.

The Celtic Church had two different expressions of martyrdom – Red martyrdom and White martyrdom. Each bore witness in a different way to the power to survive death. Red martyrdom was the actual laying down of one's life for the faith. This was always possible in the early Church and in pagan society. These martyrs often faced death singing songs of praise and praying for their persecutors. They were strong witnesses for the resurrection, that death is not a terminus, but a step on the journey to the Promised Land. The blood of such martyrs was the seed of the Church.

But there are more deaths than physical death, and they can be every bit as traumatic. For the Celts, White martyrdom was having to go into exile for the gospel's sake. To leave clan and country was to risk death at all times. It was to become homeless, even nameless. Without the security and backing of the clan, you were a nobody. It meant leaving behind all the things you trusted in. Sometimes this martyrdom was put upon someone as a penance for an evil deed or an act of violence. St Columba was made to leave Ireland because he caused so many deaths. St Patrick said that he left home and returned to Ireland to expiate the sins of youth. Others became wanderers for God – to show 'that we are pilgrims and travellers on this earth, that here we have no abiding city': on this earth there are no gilt-edged securities.

This is not a gloomy outlook on life; far from it, it calls us to a life of adventure. It can be a shaking off of false securities. No longer possessed by possessions, we may become open enough to be possessed by God. Kirkegaard has said: 'It is good once in a while to feel oneself in the hands of God, and not always eternally slinking around the familiar nooks and corners of a town where one always knows the way out.'

In what I believe to be a rather humorous expression of this, we get in the *Anglo-Saxon Chronicle* for the year 891:

> Three Scots came to King Alfred from Ireland in a boat without oars. They left their home bent on serving God in a state of pilgrimage, they did not care where. Their boat was made of two-and-a-half hides and contained enough provisions to last them seven days, and within a week came they and landed in Cornwall and shortly afterwards came to King Alfred. They were called Dubslane, Macbeth and Maelinmum.[1]

Whilst training at Kelham Theological College, I was privileged to capture a glimpse of this heroic way of living. From the 'Principles' of the Society of the Sacred Mission, I learned:

> In regard to outer things, first it is necessary that you should exercise such self-mastery that there is nothing you cannot lay easily aside. You must leave all one day whether you will or not . . .
>
> If you have given your whole life to God, why should you prefer to lose it in this way rather than that? . . .
>
> If it cost you your life, what better could you ask than that the time of trial be short, since the reward is the same?[2]

This attitude to life, far from impoverishing it, enriches it, frees it and makes it heroic. It is a way of looking at life more honestly and clearly and not getting caught with the false 'securities' of the world. We, in the twentieth century, need to recapture a vision of living daringly for our Lord, casting away our man-made securities and putting our trust in Him. We have been fooled into pretending we are self-sufficient and self-reliant. We are in danger of being 'the self-made man who worships his creator'. Perhaps we should remind ourselves where it all ends: *memento mori*, 'for death, there is no remedy in the garden.'

Now we are looking at a forbidden subject. Death is one of the taboos of our age. It is because we refuse to face it and its consequences that it has such a grip on many. We avoid not only the 'red' death, but the 'white' death, the 'change and decay' that is all around us. We work so hard at keeping things alive that should be allowed to die decently. We keep organisations alive that have passed their usefulness; we spend millions of pounds trying to sustain a past that is gone. We cover up with euphemisms and cosmetics. What we avoid at all costs is breakdown, which is looked upon as death. Breakdown is talked of in hushed tones, as if it were a deadly sin. There are countless people avoiding breakdown by tranquillising themselves one way or another. Breakdown often occurs when an old way of life or a relationship dies and we refuse to face it. We use our energies and resources to discover the 'good old days' and we are not at ease in the present. Being not at ease is often the precipitating factor of dis-ease, and disease can lead to death.

Look to the Cross. Jesus saw it coming, but He did not run away. He faced death, and the many deaths that flesh is heir to. He knew that a loved one would betray Him. He was betrayed with a kiss, deserted by His closest companions, disowned by His friend on whom He relied, left alone (yet not alone). He suffered mental, physical and spiritual agonies. He was crucified, dead and buried. His life could seem a complete breakdown, a total failure. But the Cross is empty. Breakdown is not the end. It is only part of the process of this earth. Without the cross there is no resurrection; without death, no newness of life. Without breakdown there is no breakthrough.

Too often I keep things that should be scrapped. I have an old petrol-driven lawn mower that costs me hours in repairs and money. I need to admit that it has broken down, instead of thinking it is breaking down. I need to admit it, so that I can renew it. So it is with life. We must say something is broken down; only then can it be repaired or renewed. So often it is not a breakdown we are having, but a breakthrough. If only we would see it, we are hesitating on the very edge of a new world for us. Stop saying, 'I'm having a breakdown'; say 'I have already broken down and am experiencing a break-through.' Accept that our cross, breakdown, is necessary. It will come to us, but it is only a stage on the journey and so becomes a breakthrough. So death is a gateway to glory.

Once, when visiting someone who was obviously dying, I asked her if she was afraid. Obviously she feared pain, losing a grip on life, the loss of human dignity, she was afraid of the unknown. But what she feared most was being left completely alone. She said,

'Any pain is bearable' – I thought that a very brave statement – 'but I fear being left completely alone.' Separation from others was more fearful than anything. This is still the hardest thing for many who are in hospital. It is not the approaching 'end', but the loneliness of the side-ward. I do not believe that we should leave people to face that 'great adventure' alone.

We are not alone. He is with us. Underneath are the everlasting arms – and those hands have the imprint of the nails. Right at the centre of the Christian faith is the Cross. There at the hub is a young man who has suffered injustice and all the hells that this world could hurl at Him. He is the scorned and rejected, and knows our sorrows.

With the dying person, I explored what Jesus suffered. It is amazing how much can be paralleled with what happens to us. He also had gone through it all, and triumphed. He is now alive and calls, 'Come to me.' One of the last, clear statements from that dear lady was, 'I do not know where I am going or what will be there, but I know Who is coming to meet me.'

Here are lines from various Hebridean prayers:

Through Christ's crucifying tree,
Injury come not to me; . . .
Nor oppression may I see,
King of Glory leading me.

O thou Christ upon the tree,
All my hope I place in Thee.

May the cross of the crucifixion Tree
Where the wounded back of Christ we see,
Deliverance grant from distress to me,
From death, from spell-binding to keep me free.[3]

These are not charms against evil. They are affirmations that 'through the strength of His crucifixion and burial, we arise today.' The Cross loses its meaning if it is used like a charm to escape reality – or if it becomes so overlaid with gold and silver that it is only a thing of beauty. The Cross is the promise that God cares and is involved with us in all of life, and there is nowhere where He has not been. The Cross is the way to glory.

It was getting near home time and a storm had begun. One little lass had a long way to go down dark lanes. I worried for her and asked if I should go with her. She refused my help with a smile. 'There was no need, she would be all right, she was not afraid.' It was only at the last minute that I could relax, for her father arrived to take her home. She came over to me. 'I knew daddy was coming for me and he has brought me a new coat.' I watched them as they walked out the door together, she looked so radiant.

Much later I realised what marvellous picture this was of the Christian facing death. We cannot avoid the storm or the dark, but we are not alone and we shall be given a 'new coat'. We may not know what lies ahead, but we know *Who*.

'Yea, though I walk through the valley of the shadow . . .I will fear no evil; for thou art with me.'[4]

EXERCISES

1. Know that He was crucified and lives, walks with you. Let Him walk into your past.

He walks into rooms that we thought locked indeed, that He may bring peace.

Experience that peace, His forgiveness and His living presence. He accepts you as you are.

Offer Him your failures and frustrations:
>   all that you wish to forget,
>   all that you cannot forgive,
>   all that hurts and pains you.

Walk into areas that seem to be breaking down and know that He offers you His Presence, Resurrection and Life.

Know that *nothing* can separate us from the love of God in Christ Jesus.

2. Look at the sufferings of Jesus: Betrayal . . . desertion . . . denial . . . being alone . . . physical pain . . . a feeling of injustice . . . mockery . . . agony . . . death.
Find parallels in your own life. Know that in Him we are 'more than conquerors'.

3. Meditate on Psalm 23 – 'The Lord is my Shepherd.' Make an affirmation by reading very slowly, giving meaning to each word. The Lord *is* my Shepherd . . . Then read Matthew 8.23–7.

PAUSE   Be still and know that He is God and that He is present . . . peace . . . etc . . .

PICTURE   A calm lake, beauty, a lovely place.
Allow a storm to hit it. A violent storm.
The waves are wild, the wind is fierce.
Trees are bending, branches breaking.
It gets dark. Things get worse.

Things are really out of control. *Chaos.*
Then . . .
A still small voice.
It pierces the storm and somehow triumphs over it.

Peace be still.
And there was a great calm.
Who would have believed it a minute ago?
It was like the end of the world . . . everything
doom and disaster and
now
the still waters.

PONDER   This is not a picture of a lake. It is my life.
Stormy, tempestuous, violent.
Strange, unpredictable winds blow.
Many a time we are in danger of sinking.
So many storms are because we 'go it alone'.
We do not call upon Him. And Jesus sleeps.

'O what peace we often forfeit,
O what needless pain we bear,
All because we do not carry
Everything to God in prayer.'

'Save us, Lord!' they said 'We are about to die!'
Wake Him.
Call upon Him.
Know that He is the Lord and Saviour.

PROMISE   To wake His Presence in my life.
To call upon Him in my need: 'To Thy Cross I
look and live.'
Affirm: 'With Jesus in my vessel I can smile
amid the storm.'

PRAYER   'Lord Jesus, the sea is so large and our boat is
so small.'
'Lord, save us or we perish.'

I arise today
Through the strength of his death and burial.

Circle me Lord
Keep protection near
And danger afar

Circle me Lord
Keep hope within
Keep doubt without

Circle me Lord
Keep light near
And darkness afar

Circle me Lord
Keep peace within
Keep evil out

The Trinity

The Trinity
Protecting me
The Father be
Over me
The Saviour be
Under me
The Spirit be
About me
The Holy Three
Defending me
As evening come
Bless my home
Holy Three
Watching me
As shadows fall
Hear my call
Sacred Three
Encircle me
So it may be
Amen to Thee
Holy Three
About me

O raise thou me heavenward,
great Power of my power.

———

I had been given a bicycle. It was old, gearless and rather dilapidated, but to me it was a treasure. I believed I had boundless energy and could go anywhere. I cycled the four miles from Alnwick to the coast and back, it was quite easy. So with another twelve-year-old, for that was my age, I planned to cycle to Berwick and back. This was a distance of thirty-two miles there and another thirty-two miles back. Obviously we had not calculated what this would take out of us in terms of time or energy. We just said we were going out for a little ride and a picnic. By the time we arrived at the bridge over the river Tweed to enter Berwick, we were both fearful of our mistake. We knew then we had overdone it. We only just crossed the bridge and entered the edge of the town and turned around. We had come too far and knew we would need every ounce of energy if we were to get home safely. Legs ached and refused to work properly. I was exhausted, would soon not be able to go any further. My friend was very much in the same state, we were both ready to collapse.

About four miles out of Alnwick, I got off my bike and could not remount it. I could not even walk with it. Now I experienced for myself what the Chinese mean when they say, 'If you have a journey of a hundred miles, when you have done ninety-nine miles you are only half way.' I could not go on. No amount of will power would push on my tired limbs, I had gone too far. My friend left me and went on ahead. For the last few miles I had been too much of a drag on him. I was now alone, frightened and tearful. It began to get dark. No one seemed to notice me. I thought I would die. Then suddenly, in his wagon, my father appeared. My friend had gone and told him of my plight. He got out of his cab and jumped down to me. He lifted my bike on to the back of the wagon. Then he lifted me into the passenger seat. Within minutes I was safely home and being cared for. I knew what it was to be loved and to be rescued when all my powers had gone.

This event would provide me with many images later in life. I knew what it was to have a father who would come out to meet me. I knew that when I was weary and powerless he came down to where I was and lifted me. I knew that I was not left alone, because I was loved. It was much later on that I came across a promise from God in Isaiah that suggested He would do the same: 'Even to your old age, I am he; and even to hoar hairs will I carry you: I have made, and I will bear; even I will carry, and will deliver you.'[5]

It has taken me a long time to realise that God does not need my support, rather it is I who need His. God does not need me to carry Him around, but there are certainly times when I need to be lifted by Him. I learned to pray each evening:

Support us, O Lord, all the day long of this troublous life, until the shades lengthen, and evening comes, the busy world is hushed, the fever of life is over, and our work on earth is done. Then, Lord, in Thy mercy, grant us a safe lodging, a holy rest, and peace at the last: through Jesus Christ our Lord.[6]

The request was to make me aware of the fact of the support and the uplifting power of God. So often in this life we are like a child with a load to carry, or a weighty burden to lift, we are dragged down by it. We strain and we stress, perhaps we sweat and we swear, but alone the burden is bigger than us, and we are unable to lift it.

We may with our own strength carry it for a good while, but it will get us down in the end. If we are adventuring there are times when we will find ourselves beyond our physical limits; if this never happens we really must wonder if we are trying to live life to the full. Once beyond those limits we discover that 'we have no power of ourselves to help ourselves.' We are not self-sufficient, even though we may like to give the appearance that we are. None of our powers are limitless, left to ourselves we run out of energies. We learn that we need help from outside, from a power that is greater than our power. Now, all the time the Father has been watching and waiting, wanting to help us. He has been calling to us and offering to help us. All we need do is to call upon Him and trust Him. He will carry our load for us. More than that – if need be, He will carry us also.

As another of my regular evening prayers I say, 'Into Thy hands, O Lord, I commend my spirit.' As the darkness comes, I commit myself to Him who is the light. I who have wandered all day, return home to the Father, and put myself in His keeping. I have also learned to pray this prayer whenever darkness or tiredness comes, whenever I feel confused or lost. Only recently I have started to use it at the beginning of the day. Too often I have gone on to the point of exhaustion, piling burden upon burden, before I call upon Him. Too often I have allowed myself to enter deep darkness before I have the sense to call upon the Light. I have suffered many 'deaths' before I have come to Him who is the Resurrection. There is a strange perverseness in us that prevents us from turning to Him, and making our homecoming. Though God calls, we still stall. It seems that He still comes unto his own, and His own receive Him not. This is expressed well in a modern poem:

I am the great sun, but you do not see me,
    I am your husband, but you turn away.
I am the captive, but you do not free me.
    I am the captain you will not obey.

I am the truth, but you will not believe me,
    I am the city where you will not stay,
I am your wife, your child, but you will leave me,
    I am that God to whom you will not pray.

I am your counsel, but you will not hear me,
    I am the lover whom you will betray,
I am the victor, but you will not cheer me,
    I am the holy dove whom you will slay.

I am your life, but if you will not name me,
Seal up your soul with tears, and never blame me.[7]

Let me remember, for all His Power God will not force Himself upon us. We must invite Him into our lives. We need to let His Power come to work on our power. We must allow Him who is the Resurrection and the Life to enter into our many deaths, that we may experience the resurrection now. We need to know that He comes to us so that we may have life and have it more abundantly.[8] This means letting Him enter the darkness and allowing Him to descend into our own hells. There are places in our lives where we all need Him to walk; we need His healing touch, His words of forgiveness, His liberating power. In the words of Gerard Manley Hopkins we all must

Let him easter in us, be a dayspring to the dimness in us.[9]

We must let Him transform our winter into spring, our darkness into light. Let Him come down to where we are and lift us up:

O raise thou me heavenward, great Power of my power.

Once again, this leads to the image of the Good Shepherd who is willing to lay down His life for the sheep, and who will go after that which is lost until He finds it. The Good Shepherd who is ever seeking those who err and stray. He it is who walks through the valley of the shadow of death. He it is who descends into the dark: 'He descended into hell.' The Good Shepherd enters all the hells of this world, seeking out that which is lost, and we are promised that He will not give up until He finds it. In our very weariness is the call of God, who knows His sheep and calls them by name. He comes down to where we are. But He comes down that He may lift us up: 'And when he has found it, he lays it on his shoulders, rejoicing. And when he comes home, he calls together his friends and his neighbours, saying to them, Rejoice with me, for I have found my sheep which was lost.'[10]

The uplifting power of God is something to accept and rejoice in as part of His love. We need to know that He ascended so that we might also ascend: He rose so that we might also rise. George Herbert, in his poem entitled 'Easter' begins:

Rise, heart, thy Lord is risen. Sing his praise
Without delayes
Who takes thee by the hand, that thou, likewise
With him mayst rise.

It was for this that he came down, to lift us up. At the festival of the Annunciation the Orthodox Church has these words as part of Matins:

Today is revealed the mystery that is from all
    eternity,
The Son of God becomes the Son of Man;
Sharing in that which is lower,
He makes me share in what is higher.

Not long after writing down these words, I watched a practice rescue by RAF Boulmer in Northumberland. The helicopter was hovering over a very stormy sea and trying to maintain a fixed position. In the sea was a 'person' needing rescue. The waters were icy cold and the person in them would not survive all that long. The winchman was lowered from the safety of the helicopter into the cold North Sea. But it was for a purpose; he came down to lift up; he descended to raise the perishing to safety, to save them from death. I saw here a wonderful image of the incarnation, the resurrection and the ascension: 'Now that he ascended, what is it but that he also descended first into the lower parts of the earth? He that descended is the same also that ascended up far above all heavens, that he might fill all things.'[11]

He came down to where we are so that we should not perish. He came down to lift us up. When we are set in the stormy seas of life, He is also there, waiting and wanting to help us. So I can pray with Oscar Wilde:

Come down, O Christ, and help me! Reach thy hand,
For I am drowning in a stormier sea
Than Simon on thy lake of Galilee.[12]

Now I have an image of the disciples in such a stormy sea. Jesus has gone high into the mountains to pray, He wants to be alone, with the Father in prayer. The disciples are down below and travelling across the waters. For a while all is calm and bright – then the storm comes. Like many of the storms of life it is quite unexpected. Dark clouds and great waves descend on them from nowhere. Suddenly the disciples know they are in trouble and even they, with all their experience, feel powerless. But they are not alone, He sees their need. Jesus comes down from on high, down from where He was. He enters their situation, He goes into the storm. Somehow He walks in it and it does not defeat Him. It is His presence that brings a new peace. Such an awareness can make disciples foolish, Peter thinks he can do what Jesus alone can do, he tries to walk above the waves. For a little while it seems possible, and then, naturally, he begins to sink. What else would you expect? We can often ride out a storm, triumph over great waves; but not forever. Then Jesus reaches out. He who has come down lifts Peter up. Peter will not perish because he is not alone, so Peter will triumph over the waves.

Julian of Norwich had such an image in mind when she wrote:

> He said not: 'Thou shalt not be tempest-tossed; thou shalt not be work-weary; thou shalt not be distressed'. But he did say: 'Thou shalt not be overcome.'[13]

What a wonderful statement that is for us who are in the storms of life: we will not escape the storms in this world, but we need not be overcome by them. We are not offered an easy way, out, but we are offered the Power to survive. Nor is this some impersonal power, it is the very Presence of God. Gerard Manley Hopkins expressed it in a different way:

> I admire thee, master of the tides,
>   Of the Yore-flood, of the years fall . . .
>   Ground of being, and granite of it: past all
>   Grasp God, throned behind
> Death with a sovereignty that heeds but hides,
>   bodes but abides:
>
>   With a mercy that outrides
>   The all of water, an ark
> For the listener; for the lingerer with a love glides
>   Lower than death and the dark . . .
> Our passion-plunged giant risen,

> The Christ of the Father compassionate, fetched in
> the storm of his strides.[14]

Once again Isaiah, who tells of a God who will carry, tells of a God who says:

> Fear not: for I have redeemed thee, I have called thee by thy name; thou art mine. When thou passest through the waters, I will be with thee; and through the rivers, they shall not overflow thee: when thou walkest through the fire, thou shalt not be burned; neither shall the flame kindle upon thee.[15]

Here is a God who gives power for our journey through life. Like Moses, we need to become aware of the Presence that goes with us, and that He promises to give us rest.[16] Once again we need get our imagination to work, so that we can appropriate for ourselves what is really being offered to us.

One of the ways the Celtic Christian did this was to have a series of journeying prayers. These can be seen as an extension of such statements as, 'Yea, though I walk through the valley of the shadow of death, I will fear no evil, for thou art with me.' Time and time again we need to affirm what is in fact the reality that is all around us. Too often we allow our vision to become fogged or narrowed; we need to re-tune to the Presence and Power about us. We need to know that 'as many as receive Him, to them gives He the power to become the sons (and daughters) of God.' Somehow we have to add the eternal to our perspective of life. It is for this reason that the Hebridean Christian prayed:

> God be shielding thee by each dropping sheer,
> God make every pass an opening appear,
> God make to thee each road a highway clear,
>   And may he take thee in the clasp
>   Of his own two hands' grasp.[17]

The Celtic Christians affirmed that they were always in the hands of God. No matter to what depths life descended, they knew that underneath are the everlasting arms. These hands that would bear them up, are the hands that bear the imprint of the nails. The Power-full God is a God of the passion and of compassion. He knows all the hells and torments of this world, so He is well able to come to our aid. He is there already, wanting to help us: He always stands alongside us, never leaving or forsaking us.

> God before me, God behind,
> God above me, God below;
> On the path of God I wind,
> God upon my track doth go.
>
> Who is there upon the shore?
> Who is there upon the wave?
> Who is there on sea-swell roar?
> Who is there by door-post stave?
> Who along with us doth stand?
> God and Lord on either hand.
>
> I am here abroad, without,
> I am here in want, in need,
> I am here in pain, in doubt,
> I am here in straits indeed,
> I am here alone, afraid.
> O God grant to me thine aid.[18]

Whatever our condition, our state of body or mind, He is the God who comes. He is the God who lifts us up, who rescues us from hell. Let us learn to come to Him and experience resurrection now. His Presence is a source of joy and of courage. Let us learn to say,

O raise thou me heavenward, great Power of my power.

EXERCISES

1. Learn to accept the gifts He offers with His Presence. Say slowly this verse from St Patrick's Breastplate, and mean every bit of it:

I bind unto myself today
The power of God to hold and lead,
His eye to watch, His might to stay,
His ear to hearken to my need.
The wisdom of my God to teach,
His hand to guide, His shield to ward,
The word of God to give me speech,
His heavenly host to be my guard.

2. READ
Read the story of the Lost Sheep (Luke 15.4–7).

RUMINATE
Chew the story over. See the sheep wandering off, getting further and further away. The night comes down and it is in a dangerous place. See the sheep slips over the edge of the cliff and on to a ledge. There is no way it can get back of its own accord. There are great briars that wrap themselves around it and trap it. The sheep will die there if it is left alone. Many have perished in such a spot. Already the shepherd has missed it and set off to find it. He calls it by name. The journey is long and dark. At last he hears its feeble cry. He has to descend the cliff where it has fallen. He has to go to where it is. The briars tear at his hands and feet, his head is also torn. But he goes on, he descends right into the mess it is in. He rescues it at great cost to himself. Some would say the sheep was not worth his effort – but he loves it. See how gently he lifts it. The journey back is slow and hard for the shepherd, the sheep is being carried. He

comes back rejoicing and saying to all he meets, 'Rejoice with me, for I have found my sheep which was lost.'

See this as a mirror of yourself and your actions. You are the wanderer, you are the one who has got lost. You have 'erred and strayed like a lost sheep'. Picture yourself in the ravine and in the dark. Know it is a dangerous place and that you cannot rescue yourself. You may even be in such a situation now. Listen in the silence and in the dark, for He calls His sheep by name. He is calling upon you. Let Him hear you respond. Call His Name. Repeat such words as 'Abba, Father', or 'Jesus, Saviour', or 'Spirit, Lifegiver'. Say these words over and over, knowing that He comes to you. Let the light enter your darkness. Let the Good Shepherd lift you out of where you are and bring you to a safe place. Rest in His arms and in His love.

Resolve that you will not stay in the darkness, nor will you let yourself be trapped and alone. Whenever the darkness descends, promise that you will call upon Him who calls you by name.

3. Following the last idea of being lost and raised, you may like to use the words of Christina Rossetti:

I have no wit, no words, no tears;
My heart within me like a stone
Is numbed too much for hopes or fears.
Look right, look left, I dwell alone;
I lift mine eyes, but dimmed with grief
No everlasting hills I see;
My life is in the falling leaf.
O Jesus, quicken me.

My life is like a faded leaf,
My harvest dwindled to a husk:
Truly my life is void and brief
And tedious in the barren dusk:
My life is like a frozen thing,
No bud nor greenness can I see
Yet rise it shall – the sap of Spring
O Jesus, rise in me.[19]

4. PRAY:

O God, who knowest us to be set in the midst of so many
and great dangers, that by reason of the frailty of our
nature we cannot always stand upright . . . support us in
all dangers and carry us through all temptations:
through Jesus Christ our Lord.[20]

Lift Us Lord

Into the stormy sea
You descended and lifted Peter.

Into the storms of sickness
You descended and lifted Jairus's daughter.

Into the storms of madness
You descended and lifted Legion.

Into the storms of death
You descended and lifted Lazarus.

Into the storms of hell
You descended and lifted us all.

Lift us Lord,
> From darkness to light
> From sickness to health
> From distress to calm.

Lift us Lord,
> From sadness to joy
> From fear to faith
> From loneliness to love.

Lift us Lord,
> In mind and in spirit
> In word and in deed
> In body and in soul.

Forgive Us Lord

Between me and each evil deed
Come Lord Jesus

Between me and each sinful act
Come Lord Jesus

Between me and each wicked thought
Come Lord Jesus

Between me and each wrong desire
Come Lord Jesus

The Cross between me and all ill
The Cross to foil the devil's skill

The Cross between me and all harm
The Cross to foil all evil's charm

Jesus Saviour of us all
Give us forgiveness as we call
Help us forget the evil past
Give us a hope that will last
From wicked ways may we abstain
Avoid the deeds that give Thee pain

Christ in forgiveness to me be near
Christ in forgiveness come appear
Christ in forgiveness drive off the foe
Christ in forgiveness help me below
Christ in forgiveness give me release
Christ in forgiveness I need thy peace

Enfolding

The Sacred Three
My force field be
Surrounding me
On land or sea.
Defend my kin
Keep peace within
Let darkness cease
Till soul's release.
The Sacred Three
My force field be
Ever to eternity
God enfolding me
On land or sea.

Father, I am lost and lonely.
Hold me with your hand
Guide me by your grace
Lift me by your might
Save me by your strength
Enfold me in your love.

For Aid

We bring (*name*) in weakness
For your strengthening

We bring (*name*) in sickness
For your healing

We bring (*name*) in trouble
For your calming

We bring (*name*) who is lost
For your guidance

We bring (*name*) who is lonely
For your love

We bring (*name*) who is dying
For your resurrection

The Cross of Christ

The Cross of Christ
Upon your brow
The Cross of Christ
Protect you now

The Cross of Christ
Upon your mind
The Cross of Christ
Make you kind

The Cross of Christ
Upon your head
The Cross of Christ
Save from dread

The Cross of Christ
Upon your face
The Cross of Christ
Give you grace

The Cross of Christ
Upon your heart
The Cross of Christ
Set you apart

The Cross of Christ
Upon your soul
The Cross of Christ
Keep you whole

Your Presence

Grant me your Presence
In my gasping breath.
Grant me your Presence
In the hour of death.
Grant me your Presence
In my great agony.
Grant me your Presence
Through to eternity.
Grant me your Presence
At the last dark deep.
Grant me your Presence
At the final sleep.
Grant me your Presence
At the long sigh.
Grant me your Presence
Till I come on high.
Grant me your Presence
When the world is past.
Grant me your Presence
When I rest at last.

202

High king of heaven, thou heaven's bright Sun,
O grant me its joys after vict'ry is won;
great Heart of my own heart, whatever befall,
still be thou my vision, thou Ruler of all.

———

Once when I went camping with a group of friends I wandered off as the sun was setting. I walked a good distance and did not realise how quickly it would get dark. I found the journey back full of shadows and shapes. I was full of fears and beginning to feel that I was very much on my own and lost. The darkness began to close in around me. Everything looked very black indeed. I was now near to tears, with strong feelings of insecurity and inferiority to the powers around me. Then I saw it – a tent lit up in the darkness of the night. With a lantern inside, the tent glowed in the dark. I could see shadowy outlines of familiar shapes. I was not alone, I was among friends; their light was leaking through the tent to guide me to them.

It was years later that this experience of my early teens would help me to understand something of the 'glory of God'. I would hear about 'the glory being tabernacled amongst us': that God 'pitched His tent among us'. I wondered if, in the dark nights of the desert, the tent of meeting had a guiding light within it – a light that said that the darkness is being conquered, for God dwells with us. I felt that I began to see what Moses was aiming at when he had a tent pitched for God: here in their midst was an abiding Presence. When they travelled, this was a sign that the Almighty travelled with them. When the darkness descended, here was the pillar of fire to guide them. From such a place glimpses of glory were possible: here they no longer felt insecure or inferior, for a mighty Power was at hand.

Moving on to the New Testament, I realised that in Jesus, God has become tabernacled amongst us in a special way. 'The Word was made flesh and dwelt among us, and we beheld His glory.' For those with eyes to see, whose vision is cleared, in Jesus we get our clearest glimpse of the Divine. Not only is this a glimpse, it is the assurance that He dwells among us. We can also discover that he is the light that shines in our darkness; He is the light of the world. In the Advent season, as the days get dark, I thrill to the words of the blessing from the Alternative Service Book: 'Christ the Sun of righteousness shine upon you and scatter the darkness from before your path.' I know there is a play on words between 'son' and 'sun', and I like it; without either there would be no life for us. Both are the light of the world. Zacharias rejoiced in the coming of Jesus with the words, 'Through the tender mercy of our God ... the dayspring from on high has visited us, to give light to them that sit in darkness and in the shadow of death, and to guide our feet into the way of peace.'[21]

I was to learn time and time again, because He is tabernacled among us, that His Presence shines through His creation. We may only see through a glass darkly, but we do see hints of His being there, and glimpses of the Divine. There are times in our lives when our senses are cleansed, when we become more still, and we are aware of the great Other. We should learn to look over our experiences and say with awe, 'We beheld his glory . . .' or with Jacob, 'Surely the Lord is in this place and I knew it not.' Perhaps, like Moses, we will have to devise a tent of meeting, a fixed place and a fixed time where we seek to get glimpses of glory. Here we will sit in quiet and, to use the words of John Donne, we can 'tune the instrument at the gate'. We need to train our senses so that they are more aware of Him who comes. Here at our tent of meeting we shall

seek to 'let go and let God', we shall leave all aside to let
Him fill our moments and our days. We shall seek rest
from our striving and let Him be our power and our
peace. Here we shall seek to speak to God face to face,
as a man does with his friend. Here we shall look over
our day to capture a vision of God in our midst.

Let it be said that most of us will not see God, but all of
us can experience Him. If you read the book of Exodus
chapter 33 verses 7 to 23, you will discover that what we
have been talking about was experienced by Moses. For
all the 'tent of the Lord's Presence' and the promise
from God, 'I will go with you and give you victory',
Moses asked to see the dazzling light of God's Presence.
But he was told that a man can have only a glimpse of
the Divine, for 'no one can see God and live.' What we
are offered are signs of the Presence. The numinous is
that which nods to us, that attracts us through and in
Creation. It is a lovely thought that God is on a nodding
relationship with us – and that He leaves signs of His
presence for us to discover. The discovery may be only
momentary, like a flash in the dark, but it gives us
strength for our journey and hope for the future.
Because I have travelled long dark nights on lonely
roads, I am very fond of this description from Tom
Stoppard's *Jumpers*:

How does one know what it is one believes when it's
so difficult to know what one knows? I cannot claim
to know that God exists, I only claim that he does
without my knowing it, and while I claim as much I
do not claim to know as much; indeed I cannot know
and God knows I cannot. (*Pause*) And yet I tell you
that, now and again, not necessarily in the contemplation of rainbows or new-born babies, nor in the
extremities of pain and joy, but probably ambushed
by some quite trivial moment – say the exchange of

signals between two long-distance lorry-drivers in the black sleet of a god-awful night on the old A1 – then in that dip-flash, dip-flash of headlights in the rain that seems to affirm some common ground that is not animal and not long-distance lorry-driving – then I tell you I know.[22]

How often I have seen that flash of lights without seeing a person, yet knowing that beyond the lights is a familiar friend or a fellow-traveller. The flashing lights are not the presence but a sign of the presence, and a hint of the greater Presence beyond. Again and again this Presence calls out through the multitude of things. The poets often speak of this Presence ever near and breaking into our lives. We can all experience with Gerard Manley Hopkins that:

> The world is charged with the grandeur of God.
> It will flame out, like shining from shook foil.[23]

A Presence can suddenly break into our darkness and shatter our blindness. This Presence is ever seeking us out, desiring to cure our deafness. Always wanting us to come home to the light and love of our Maker. Time and time again God calls and, so often, we are the one who stalls. But because He is ever near there is no hiding place from Him. The 'three person'd God' will continue to 'batter our heart' to seek admission. Often it is when we least expect it that the Presence breaks through. This was put forcibly in Robert Browning's 'Bishop Blougram's Apology'.

> Just when we're safest, there's a sunset-touch,
> A fancy from a flower-bell, some one's death,
> A chorus-ending from Euripides,
> And that's enough for fifty hopes and fears . . .
> As old and new at once as nature's self,
> To rap and knock and enter in our soul.

In a sunset, in a song, in a shop, in a saint, in the sun or in the Son, God seeks us out and draws us to Himself. I once felt this in a great congregation, the first time I heard Handel's *Messiah*. I was moved time and time again by the music and words. Great themes enveloped the church; passion and pain, pastoral love and peace all seemed to surround us and fill us. The air was vibrant and expectant, with a feeling that there was something else, something special, still to come. The enthusiasm of the singers was infectious. Suddenly we were all caught up in the rapture of the Hallelujah Chorus, praising the 'King of kings, and Lord of lords, forever and ever'. This proclamation echoed and reverberated all around us and within us. I wanted to be part of it, to join in. I felt that we were being allowed a glimpse of eternity, of the worship of God, of His Glory. We were privileged to be allowed a glimpse of the Divine.

Because of such awareness, and so many other experiences, of the God who nods to us, of the numinous, I know that life is enriched by such moments. I want others to discover it and enjoy it. This is not an experience for the privileged few but it is one we can all have. I want to repeat again and again, 'The Lord is at hand.' I feel I want to join Teilhard de Chardin when he says in his 'Mass on the World', 'I can preach only the mystery of your flesh, you the Soul shining forth through all that surrounds us.'[24]

The people of the Outer Hebrides managed to capture a feeling of this glory in so many of their prayers. Although these prayers are full of the doctrine of their beliefs, they well up from the heart and radiate out to all that is around them. There is not one area of life that is not touched by prayer and by the belief that He is there and He cares. So they begin the day with Him, and no matter what the day is like it will now hold a new brightness . . .

Though the dawn breaks cheerless on this isle
    today,
My spirit walks in a path of light
For I know my greatness.
Thou hast built me a throne within thy heart,
I dwell safely within the circle of thy care,
I cannot for a moment fall out of thine everlasting
    arms.
I am on my way to thy glory.[25]

The talking with, and singing to, God continued to give glory to their day. They had prayers for fire-lighting, walking to work, at work, in the home. They were never without their companion.

Saviour and friend, how wonderful art thou!
My companion upon the changeful way.
The comforter of its weariness.
My guide to the eternal town.
The welcome at its gate.[26]

Such prayers are created by the joy of their inner being, or are in fact the creators of that joy – a joy which comes from having a glimpse of His Glory, from knowing that our God is tabernacled among us. Time and time again, in the ordinariness of life, they rejoiced in the Lord. They took to heart the words from the letter ro the Philippians:

Rejoice in the Lord always; again I say, Rejoice . . . The Lord is at hand. Have no anxiety about anything, but in everything by prayer and supplication with thanksgiving let your requests be made known to God. And the peace of God, which passes all understanding, will keep your hearts and your minds through Christ Jesus.[27]

Not only does our anxiety subside when we know that we are not alone, but we get a new sense of victory.

We are able to triumph because we are not alone, we are not in the dark, we will not be defeated. Victory may not be yet, but through Him who loves us ultimate victory is offered to us. No matter what circumstances we find ourselves in, no matter how much goes against us, the final outcome is assured. The Christ Presence says to us, 'In the world you shall have tribulation; but be of good cheer, I have overcome the world.'[28] The whole of H. F. Lyte's hymn 'Abide with me' deserves a time of meditation on this subject: for the time being here is one verse:

> I fear no foe with thee at hand to bless:
> Ills have no weight, and tears no bitterness.
> Where is death's sting? Where grave thy victory?
> I triumph still, if thou abide with me.

This verse very much echoes St Paul in his writing to the Corinthians on the resurrection:

> Thanks be to God, who gives us the victory through our Lord Jesus Christ. Therefore, my beloved brethren, be steadfast, immoveable, always abounding in the work of the Lord, knowing that in the Lord your labour is not in vain.[29]

Some of the great mistakes of our age are about life and its triumphs or otherwise. I believe in positive thinking – but some people are positively stupid in their affirmations. There are certainly times when 'mind over matter' will not work. There is a kind of so-called 'positive thinking' that refuses to accept the reality of the situation. In the way of our world every team cannot be a winner, nor can every individual. We have to accept that, left to our own devices, there is many a battle which we will not win. In our own right we are neither almighty nor eternal. However, when we link our lives to His, we can begin to predict the outcome with some confidence. We may seem to lose every stage of the battle, but we know we have not lost the victory. We may seem to go down at every round, but we know that we shall be raised at the last.

There were words of wisdom in an old soldier friend when, asked how he was, he replied, 'Battling on'. He knew that to win a minor skirmish was not to win the campaign. He knew that victory today did not guarantee that we would win again tomorrow. That old soldier when he died knew that, through his Captain, victory was assured him, but he had also heard the victory song many times:

And when the strife is fierce, the warfare long,
Steals on the ear the distant triumph-song,
And hearts are brave again and arms are strong.
Alleluia![30]

There are some very telling words at the end of Luke's account of the temptations of Jesus: 'The devil left him for a season.' This was not the end of the fight, it was but a single round. There was no doubt that the devil would be back. We must realise that as long as we live we are part of the 'Church militant here on earth'. We are not released from the warfare, but we are guaranteed the final outcome. We need to keep our vision of Him, and know that in Him we are more than conquerors.

We need to keep our vision of the other world or we will get this one out of perspective. J. Patterson-Smyth writing of the angels when Jesus was born in Bethlehem says:

Two worlds are in the picture. Keep the whole picture in view, else the story will go wrong . . . On the earthly side just a stable, a manger, the cattle in the stalls, a woman wrapping her baby in swaddling clothes. Nothing of wonder in it. Nothing of awe.

Until the world from which He came flashes in upon the scene . . . Remember it is all one story, all one picture . . . we believe in it all right. But we are dull and slow of heart. We let it slip out of view. And so our picture gets out of focus. Unless we keep habitually in mind that other world, that eager, interested, enthusiastic world, its very wonder and beauty tend to separate it from us, to make the picture of the angels from Heaven rather misty and cloud-like beside that of the manger and the Baby on earth. Now that must not be. Any haziness as to the reality and close presence of that world puts the whole story out of gear.[31]

We need to keep a vision of this other world. Not as a place far away or set in another time, but a world that keeps breaking into our lives. Not a world that runs parallel to ours, but a world that is closely inter-woven with ours, in fact a world in which our world shares and into which we can enter. We all need to set off on a quest, like Lucy in *The Lion, the Witch and the Wardrobe*, to discover a way of entering that other world and enjoying its great riches.

There is no need for us to be apologetic about this quest, or for that matter to apologise for our belief – those who do not believe have a lot more explaining to do. For the person with even the beginnings of vision, life is ever expanding with new vistas and horizons. True, we may be diminished like other folks, but we know we shall not perish: we may be knocked down but we know we shall not be counted out: 'The supreme power belongs to God, not to us. We are often troubled but not crushed; sometimes in doubt, but never in despair; there are many enemies, but we are never without a friend; and though badly hurt at times, we are not destroyed.'[32]

We know life to be a romance, because we know that all was created by love and for love. The relationships between God, the world, others, and ourselves, all offer contacts with mystery and love. In all there is an abiding Presence that gives meaning and purpose: without this Presence all becomes futile and hollow. If only we would allow our vision to be cleansed, then I am sure the words of the Stage Manager in Thorton Wilder's play *Our Town* would prove to be true:

> We all know that something is eternal. And it ain't houses and it ain't names and it ain't even the stars – everybody knows in their bones that something is eternal and that something is to do with human beings. All the greatest people who ever lived have been telling us that for five thousand years and yet you'd be surprised how many people are always losing hold of it. There's something way down deep that's eternal about every human being.

We know that the 'eternal' in us is not ours by rights, it is a gift from God. In His love He does not want us to perish, as is our natural tendency, but to have – now – everlasting life. If there is a battle to be fought for eternal life, the outcome has already been decided in Christ our Lord. In Him we are more than conquerors. In Him a brighter dawn has broken. 'Thanks be to God, who gives us the victory.'

> *High King of heaven, thou heaven's bright Sun,*
> *O grant me its joys after vict'ry is won;*
> *great Heart of my own heart, whatever befall,*
> *still be Thou my vision, thou Ruler of all.*

EXERCISES

1. Seek to know that the Risen Lord, who descended into all the hells of this world, has conquered death, and that He is with you. Use the following hymn as a meditation:

Abide with me, fast falls the eventide:
The darkness deepens; Lord, with me abide:
When other helpers fail, and comforts flee,
Help of the helpless, O abide with me.

Swift to its close ebbs out life's little day;
Earth's joys grow dim, its glories pass away;
Change and decay in all around I see:
O thou who changest not, abide with me.

I need thy presence every passing hour;
What but thy grace can foil the tempter's power?
Who like thyself my guide and stay can be?
Through cloud and sunshine, Lord, abide with me.

I fear no foe with thee at hand to bless;
Ills have no weight, and tears no bitterness.
Where is death's sting? Where, grave, thy victory?
I triumph still, if thou abide with me.

Hold thou thy Cross before my closing eyes;
Shine through the gloom, and point me to the skies:
Heaven's morning breaks, and earth's vain shadows
    flee;
In life, in death, O Lord, abide with me.

2. Picture the Risen Lord standing before you. Seek to know that you are in His Presence. Speak to Him by name. Say, 'Jesus', and in saying His name seek to express your love. Say it again and again, to express your longing and love for Him.

Now picture someone who needs your prayers. See that He is with them. Again say, 'Jesus'. Express your love for Him and for them. Know that He is with them and offers His love. See each of them surrounded and bathed in His light. Know that in Him we triumph, and that we are all in Him. In time, move to someone else who needs your prayer and meet Jesus there, again call His name.

End this prayer with an affirmation of His love and His promise that in Him all will be well.

Christ is the morning star, Who when the night of this world is past, promises and reveals to His saints the eternal life of light. [33]

3. Make this prayer from the island of Benbecula your own.

O Being of life! O Being of peace!
O Being of time, and time without cease!
O Being, infinite, eternity!
O Being, infinite, eternity!

In good means of life be thou keeping me.
In all good intending, O keeping be,
Be keeping me always in good estate,
Far better than I know to supplicate,
    O better than I know to supplicate!

Be shepherding me for all this day long,
Relieve my distress, relieve me from wrong,
Enfold me this night with thine arms' embrace,
And pour upon me thy bountiful grace,
    O pour upon me thy bountiful grace!

My speaking and words do thou guard for me,
And strengthen for me my love, charity,
Illumine for me the stream I must o'er
And succour thou me when I pass death's door,
    O succour thou me when I pass death's door! [34]

4. Learn that:

'He is risen'
That through Him we may discover faith:
in ourselves
in our world
in our God.

'He is risen'
That in Him we may rekindle hope:
for the abandoned
for the despairing
for the dreamless.

'He is risen'
That in Him we may restore love:
to those from whom we have kept it
to those who are most near to us
to those we will never meet
to all and everything.

'He is risen.'[35]

216

Darkness

Though the mists veil the sky,
And the sun goes from on high,
Though waves roar and winds increase,
I know the mighty God is our peace.

Though the light has turned to night,
And gathering storms cause fright,
Though all around me threatens harm,
I know the saving God is our calm.

Though joy from day has passed,
And each breath feels like our last,
Though the mind feels it can't cope,
The strengthening Spirit is our hope.

The Blessed Trinity my light shall be,
With eternal life supplying me.
There is hope, my joy, my love,
Enfolded in God, I am lifted above.

Invocations

Lord hear us
Lord have mercy
Lord be with us
Lord have mercy
Lord help us
Lord have mercy

Christ save us
Christ have mercy
Christ strengthen us
Christ have mercy
Christ support us
Christ have mercy

Spirit protect us
Lord have mercy
Spirit guide us
Lord have mercy
Spirit go with us
Lord have mercy

'Let Loose in the World'

I arise today
Through the strength of his resurrection with his
  ascension.

One cold grey day, I climbed up on to the high moors.
The game keepers were up there 'burning off' the
heather, and their fire attracted me. There was a great
blaze. For a while I just enjoyed the warmth and com-
panionship. The heather was perishing in the flames; it
hissed as it burned. These men knew what they were
doing, all was planned and under control. The area for
'burning off' had been chosen carefully. The heather
here had become old and useless, all twisted and
gnarled; it had lost its sweetness and no longer sus-
tained the moorland life. So, it perished in the flames.
The game-keepers made sure the peaty soil did not
burn. After the fire, the earth would be bare, blackened,
lifeless. Then, one day, new shoots would begin to
show. The heather had not been destroyed, only its old
body. Under the peaty soil the roots had been un-
harmed and soon sweet, life-sustaining heather would
grow once more. It had not perished, but would arise,
phoenix-like, from the flames.

Here for me was a picture of the Resurrection: the old
body may be destroyed, yet the essential being will not
perish, but have everlasting life. Watching the fire, I
looked forward to the new green shoots. An old French
tune came to mind and the words, 'Love is come again'.

In the grave they laid him, Love whom men had
  slain,
Thinking that never he would wake again.
Laid in the earth, like grain that sleeps unseen:
Love is come again
Like wheat that springeth green.

Forth he came at Easter, like the risen grain
He that for three days in the grave had lain.
Quick from the dead my risen Lord is seen:
Love is come again
Like wheat that springeth green.

When our hearts are wintry, grieving or in pain,
Thy touch can call us back to life again.
Fields of our hearts that dead and bare have been:
Love is come again
Like wheat that springeth green.[36]

Leaving the game-keepers and the 'burning off', I returned home strangely warmed, not by their fire, but by the Presence of the Risen Lord. There on the moor He had come again, and for me that day was no longer dull and grey.

In many ways the Celtic Church took the Resurrection for granted, because they experienced in their lives and worship the real Presence of the Risen Lord. There was no need for them to go back continually to the tomb and puzzle over it. They were not concerned about the empty tomb, they sought their Lord among the living. They took to heart the words of Scripture spoken to the followers of Jesus: 'Why are you looking among the dead for the one who is alive? He is not here; He has been raised.'[37]

Perhaps it is no accident that there was no appearance of Christ in the tomb. He does not want us to be held in that grey area, nor to concentrate our energies there. When we are faced with the Risen Lord, to spend our time looking into an empty grave is a foolishness. Christ the Risen Lord wants us to walk with Him in the fullness of life. He is not a theory about death and survival, He is a Person to be encountered, a Presence to meet. He is the Resurrection.

It is obvious that if we do not believe in the Resurrection, we cannot have met the Risen Lord. To *not* have met the Risen Lord leaves us with theories about life and death and problems about empty tombs. We are still the wrong side of Easter Day and so miss His glory. One of the old Irish commentators, writing on 1 Corinthians 15.17, has said: 'It is manifest that unless you believe the Resurrection of Christ from among the dead, your faith will not sanctify you in that wise and will not save you from your sins.'

There is no doubt that the Resurrection is essential to our whole faith. Without His Resurrection, our faith becomes meaningless. If He is not raised, then there is no Resurrection or eternal life for us. Once we experience that He is risen, then life takes on a whole new meaning. We are no longer in the realm of theories; we are in eternal life. Patrick said in his *Confessions*:

> Without any doubt we shall rise on that day, in the clear shining of the sun, that is in the glory of Christ Jesus our Redeemer, as sons of the living God, and joint-heirs with Christ, and conformed to His image, that will be, since of Him and through Him and in Him we shall reign.

So already we begin to discover that we are the sons and daughters of God; we shall not perish but have everlasting life. We are learning that 'nothing shall separate us from the love of God'. Already we have inherited the Kingdom of Heaven.

Before the coming of Christianity, and long after the Irish talked of Tir-nan-Og 'the world of the Ever Young', this was already their feeling about life, that it could be eternal. This world was never far away, but ever close to them. This world could be stumbled upon by accident; you could be led into it by shining beings. It was there to be discovered, or seen by the mystic, though beyond the eyes of mortal men. It was this sort of feeling for eternity that made W. B. Yeats write: 'In Ireland this world and the world we go to after death are not far apart.'

It was not too difficult for the Celt to accept that 'the kingdom of heaven is at hand.' Nor was it too difficult to accept that if Christ is risen we should meet Him and let our lives intertwine. So in 'The Deer's Cry' Patrick could say:

Christ to shield me today . . .
Christ with me, Christ before me, Christ behind me.
Christ in me, Christ beneath me, Christ above me.
Christ on my right, Christ on my left,
Christ when I lie down . . . when I sit down . . .
    when I arise.

Not only the Incarnate but the Risen Christ is there to be discovered. If you asked the Celt where is Jesus now, the reply would be very similar to the one Procula received from Longinus in Masefield's play, *The Trial of Jesus*. She asked, 'Do you think he is dead?' and he replied, 'No, lady, I don't.' When asked, 'Then where is he?' Longinus replied, 'Let loose in the world, lady.'

The Risen Christ is 'let loose in the world'. This discovery was first made in the greyness of the dawn by Mary Magdalene. For two nights she had not slept well. Her eyes were red with tears and lack of rest. She had seen Him die. It was as if evil had triumphed and injustice had won the day. How cruel this world is; and that is a fact. She had heard Him cry 'Why?' from the Cross, and it seemed there was no answer. She kept asking 'Why?' but it only made her more confused. There was not even an answer from God. A great heaviness settled on Mary's heart and mind, like the stone she saw rolled against the tomb. Such a weight! She wondered if anyone could lift it. If only someone would help, if someone would roll away the stone, she would go and be with Him. She might as well go to the grave, her hope and future were gone.

Before dawn came, Mary set off, still with the nagging question, 'Who will move the stone?' Who would move the heaviness in her heart and the great stone that sealed the grave? When she arrived in the garden, the stone was already rolled away. She knew it would take a lot of strength and courage to do that. Now she would go to her Lord. But He was not there. A grave robber must have been at work. She could hardly see for her tears, her vision was blurred. There was someone there in the garden; could it be the gardener? 'Sir, they have taken away my Lord. If you know where He is . . .' It was then that the stranger turned. 'Mary', he said. It was the Lord. He had robbed the grave and death and He is let loose in the world.

He is now to be met, to be discovered in our world. He can still be found in the garden, or on the seashore. The Resurrection stories will only make sense if we still experience and affirm His Presence as a reality.

A woman on the island of Harris was a leper, and so banished to the fringes of the island, to the seashore. In her treating of herself by the use of medicinal herbs and diet, she was healed. In thanksgiving, she rejoiced in the Presence of the Risen Lord:

> There is no plant in all the land
> But blooms replete with thy virtue,
> Each form in all the sweeping strand
> With joy replete thou dost endue,
>   O Jesu, Jesu, Jesu,
>   Unto whom all praise is due.[38]

This was not a lapse into a romantic pantheism, but a seeking of strength and solace from the Risen Lord. On Barra this was expressed even more strongly:

Jesus the Encompasser

Jesu! Only-begotten mine,
God the Father's Lamb sacrificed,
Thou didst give thy body's blood-wine
From the grave-death to buy me right.
My shield, my encircler, my Christ, my Christ!
For each day, each night, for each dark, each light;
My shield, my encircler, my Christ, my Christ!
For each day, each night, for each dark, each
light.

Jesu! uphold me and be nigh,
My triumph, treasure, thou art now,
When I lie down, when stand, be by,
Whenever I watch, when I sleep.
My aid, my encircler, MacMary thou!
My strength everlasting, MacDavid, keep;
My aid, my encircler, MacMary thou!
My strength everlasting, MacDavid, keep.[39]

True strength and ability to triumph come from Him who has triumphed: 'through him, we have complete victory.'

Two people with their hopes shattered turned their backs on the Holy City. It was late in the day and they were on the road home to Emmaus. As they walked, they talked. It was then that He came, there on the ordinary road. He came as they journeyed and He walked with them. So He comes with us on our journey through life. We may not recognise Him, but He is present. We may not know what lies around the next corner, but it is our privilege to know Who it is Who goes with us.

The King to shield you in the glen,
The Christ to aid you in the ben,
Spirit to bathe you on the brae,

> Hollow, or hill, or plain your way,
> Be glen, or ben, or plain your way.[40]

When loved ones set out on a journey, to work at sea, or drive cattle overland, they are reminded of a Presence that never left them.

> Travelling the highland, travelling the townland,
>   Travelling the bogland long and wide,
> God the Son's herding round your hoofs'
>   downland,
>   Safe and whole return home to bide,
> God the Son's herding round your hoofs'
>   downland,
>   Safe and whole return home to bide.[41]

In the prayers of the Celts there are many journeying prayers that ask that we may know we are not alone, that He travels with us. Too many of us are like the travellers on the Emmaus road – our eyes are too dim to see Him. We need to learn to pray, 'Lord open my eyes, that I may see Thy risen Presence about me.'

Even though they did not recognise Him, the couple on arriving at Emmaus welcomed the 'stranger'. Here once more was the discovery that when we open our lives to the other, we give the Great Other the opportunity of coming in. At their table they made room for the unexpected guest, and there 'they recognised the Lord when he broke the bread.' A Grace before meals said on Benbecula runs:

> Be with me, O God, at breaking of bread,
> And be with me, O God, when I have fed.[42]

The Christ is still willing to sit at our table and share in our fellowship. He is still to be discovered in the 'breaking', if only we can open our eyes to His Presence. Unless Christ is at home in our home, we must really question our faith. For the Christian, faith is not a set of beliefs, but a relationship with the Risen Lord.

After a while, the disciples went fishing again on the Sea of Galilee; they returned to work. It was in that ordinary place, while they were working, that He appeared on the shore. Now He had been seen by individuals and groups; in the garden, on the road, at a meal in a living room, on the beach. Wherever they were, He came. No one returned to the tomb, for He had robbed it. They had no doubt that, whether they were in boat or barn, toiling or resting, their Lord went with them. They would naturally talk to Him, without any affectation ask Him to help them and to share their tasks. The Lord went with them and worked through them.

Too often we talk of Jesus as if He were a figure in history; we speak of what He did, what He has done, as if it were all over and finished with. We relegate Jesus to Palestine. But He is 'loose in the world'. With the Celt, we must learn to talk to Him rather than talk about Him. We must discipline ourselves so that we talk of Him in the present tense: 'Jesus is . . .' It is good to make statements and affirmations about Him in the present. Celebrate the Presence in the Present. For He is the Resurrection and He is here with us now. Today, I arise in the strength of His Resurrection.

The Ascension is the completing of the missions of Christ. He came down so that He could lift man up. He became man so that man could become Divine. The whole purpose of the Incarnation was to free us from the bonds of this world and lift us up to where He has gone before.

My favourite image of the Ascension comes from the earthly life of Jesus. Jesus is up in the mountains with the Father when a storm hits His disciples and threatens to engulf them. He comes down to where they are, to be with them in the storm. Somehow or other, though He is in the storm, He is above it. It does not swamp Him. He walks the waves. So He enters the storms and tempests of our lives. Peter is encouraged by the Presence and risks walking on the stormy water. For a while he appears to be able – it is amazing what we can achieve – but then, naturally, he begins to sink. Soon the storm will envelop him. Jesus does not let him sink into the depths; He will not let him perish. He reaches out His hand and raises him.

I know that Jesus still enters the storms of life. He comes down from the Father to lift us up. His hand raises us from that which would engulf us. When I am in the depths, I put my hand into the hand of the Risen and Ascended Lord. He lifts me out of the darkness into His own glorious light.

It was natural for the Celtic Christian to pray:

> 'Tis from my mouth that my prayer I say,
> 'Tis from my heart that my prayer I pray,
> 'Tis before thee that my prayer I lay,
> To thyself, O healing Hand, I call
> O thou Son of God who saves us all.
>
> O strengthen me in every good thing,
> In every strait thine encompassing,
> Safeguard me in every ill and pain,
> From every venom do thou restrain . . .
>
> Glorious Master of star and cloud,
> Glorious Master of the sky browed,
> Glorious Master of heav'nly place,
> O blest by thee is each tribe and race.
>
> O mayest thou for me intercede
> With the great Lord of Life indeed.[43]

Because he believes in the real Presence at the close of the day, he asks for protection of the King of Heaven, that in the morning he may ascend. If by some mischance this night sleep should turn into death, he will still arise in the power of Christ.

I am going now into the sleep,
Be it that I in health shall wake;
If death be to me in deathly sleep,
Be it that in thine own arm's keep,
O God of grace, to new life I wake;
O be it in thy dear arm's keep,
O God of grace, that I shall awake!

Be my soul on thy right hand, O God,
O thou King of the heaven of heaven;
Thou it was who didst buy with thy blood,
Thine the life for my sake was given;
Encompass thou me this night, O God,
That no harm, no mischief be given.[44]

The message is clear and simple:
   'Death is conquered. Man is free, Christ has won the
Victory.'

EXERCISES

1. Make sure you talk of a living Lord in the present
tense. Affirm: 'Jesus is . . . Jesus is alive . . . Jesus is here
. . . Jesus is life . . . Jesus is . . .'

2. The Risen and Ascended Lord is present in your life.
You cannot imagine it, but you can experience Him.
Open your life to Him and let Him walk with you.

Walk with Him into the Past, into rooms of memory, and
know that now He brings His love, His peace, His
forgiveness. In the dark places today He shines. He
comes to all those death-threatening events, in order
that we should not perish. Amid the storms of passion
He is there. Today, put your hand into the hand of God.

Walk with Him Today. This is what is most important. Do not leave Jesus in the past or in some distant future. He is here, saying, 'I will be with you always.' Invite Him into your daily life, share your journeys with Him. Let Him be there at the breaking of the bread (or the breaking of your heart). Let Him be at home in your home. Speak to Him freely and easily. Let it be seen that you have been (and are still) with Christ.

Walk with Him into the Future. Know that you never walk alone; He will not leave you nor forsake you. You may not know what lies ahead, but you know Who it is that goes with you. 'Lord Jesus, though I walk through the valley of the shadow of death, I will fear no evil: for Thou art with me.'

3.   *Lord lift me*

> Lord, from this world's stormy sea
> Give your hand for lifting me
> Lord, lift me from the darkest night
> Lord, lift me into the realm of light
> Lord, lift me from this body's pain
> Lord, lift me up and keep me sane
> Lord, lift me from the things I dread
> Lord, lift me from the living dead
> Lord, lift me from the place I lie
> Lord, lift me that I never die.

I arise today,
In the strength of his resurrection with his ascension.

The Good Shepherd

The herding of the shepherd
Keep you safe from danger
Free you from harm

The herding of the shepherd
Keep you safe from sickness
Free you from alarm

The herding of the shepherd
Keep you from despair
Have you in his care

The herding of the shepherd
Keep you from sorrow
Today and tomorrow

The shepherd's love enfold
Keep you in his hold

The shepherd's might enclasp
Keep you in his grasp

Christ our Shepherd King
Our praises to thee we sing

Good Shepherd

                    be over me to shelter me
                    under me to uphold me
                    behind me to direct me
                    before me to lead me
                    about me to protect me
                    ever with me to save me
                    above me to lift me
and bring me to the green pasture of eternal life.

Easter Blessing

The Lord of the empty tomb
The conqueror of gloom
Come to you

The Lord in the garden walking
The Lord to Mary talking
Come to you

The Lord in the Upper Room
Dispelling fear and doom
Come to you

The Lord on the road to Emmaus
The Lord giving hope to Thomas
Come to you

The Lord appearing on the shore
Giving us life for ever more
Come to you

Jesus Stood on the Shore

When morning was come
Jesus stood on the shore.[45]

Do you ever feel that you have spent all your energy for nothing, that you have worked hard for little or no reward? Perhaps the light has gone out of your life, you are lonely and in the dark. This feeling was expressed fully by a couple on holiday. They had walked down the very steep bank of a seaside village and back up again; they were weary and felt frustrated.

'All that walk for nothing,' said the man, gasping for breath.

'All the journey for nothing,' said the woman, almost in tears.

'That's life,' said the man as they travelled on in their trivial pursuits.

Every now and again it is as if some great tide has ebbed and we are once more at a low.

This low tide is expressed in many different ways in history and often by the poets. Here is a piece from an Anglo-Saxon poem called 'The Seafarer':

He who lives most prosperously on land does not understand how I, careworn and cut off from my kinsmen, have as an exile endured a winter on the icy sea.[46]

Then again those lines from the 'Ancient Mariner':

. . . this soul hath been
Alone on a wide, wide sea;
So lonely 'twas, that God himself
Scarce seemed there to be.

Certainly the Psalmist was right: *Nisi Dominus frustra*. Without the Lord all frustrates. It is as if some great ebb tide was determined to strip every thing bare.

PICTURE
So it was with the disciples; they had toiled all night and taken nothing. Try and see them in the dark, frustrated.

232

They had travelled for three years with Jesus, expecting a new occupation. Here they were back fishing, back in the dark. They were working hard but achieving nothing. It is not difficult to visualise this situation. Not only nets, but life, seemed empty. There was the nagging feeling that the dull preacher was right when he said, 'Vanity, vanity, all is in vain.' What a way to end their days, toiling in the dark!

Picture it well; you have been there before and will be there again. Life has a habit of suddenly ebbing and laying life bare. There is a feeling, for some of the disciples at least, that they have been here before. This is not an experience that is uncommon to them. This emptiness reverberates with other times, life seems to be repeating itself. Picture them there in the dark, weary, catching nothing. Then watch the dawn come. Even now the tide is flowing on another shore. Picture the bareness being covered, the emptiness being filled. Learn to anticipate and to wait. Know that morning will come.

When morning was come, Jesus stood on the shore.

The dawn has a habit of coming suddenly – though some will aver that 'the darkest moments come just before the dawn.' Picture the disciples suddenly being flooded with light, the sky is blue and the day is bright. The mists are rising on the shore – and there He is, part hidden, wrapped in the morning mist. It would be easy not to notice Him, but He is there.

Jesus stands on the shore waiting for us to come to Him, gently beckoning to us. He calls us through our darkness and frustrations. The low tide reveals the shore – and Jesus standing there. The disciples enter a new day, new life, and new opportunities with their Lord.

PRESENCE
Know that He is there in your darkness.

Know that, though the mists hide Him, he stands

233

waiting on the shore and that He is gently calling you.
Say:

> You Lord are in this place
> Your Presence fills it
> Your Presence is light.

In His Presence know that the darkness rolls away.
There is a great brightness seeking to enter our lives.
Will we still cling to the shadows? Are we determined to
stay in the dark? The sun is rising, 'new perils past, new
sins forgiven, new thoughts of God, new hopes of
heaven'.

See that He is with you. Even when the tide has ebbed
Jesus can be found on the shore. When resources are
low, renewal is still being offered us. Somewhere
within our darkness a brighter dawn seeks to break.
Are we able to open our eyes and our minds to the
Presence? He is there, where the water meets the land,
where the land meets the skies, where the darkness is
turning to light, where the temporal is becoming
eternal. He is there at each meeting place, every shore
of this world – and the shores of eternity.

Even now He waits on you to recognise Him.

He waits on you to turn to Him.

He waits for the darkness to clear and the mists to lift.

He bids us come.

Be refreshed.

Renewed.

Restored.

Lord, open my eyes that I may see – your Presence
now and eternally.

PONDER

Think upon these words from Alistair Maclean's *Hebridean Altars*:

> I say to myself each night, 'The dawn will come and all
> this dark will be gone.' I watch the tide's far ebb and
> whisper, 'It will flow.' In the mid of winter I cry to my
> heart, 'Soon the green banners of spring will blow
> through the land.' Yet surer still I am that Thou art my

friend. For Thou hast wrought a miracle in my thought. Thou has changed faith to knowledge, and hope to sight.[47]

Also think upon and pray these words from the same book:

Though the dawn breaks cheerless on this Isle today, my spirit walks upon a path of light.
For I know my greatness.
Thou hast built a throne within Thy heart.
I dwell safely within the circle of Thy care.
I cannot for a moment fall out of Thine everlasting arms:
I am on my way to Thy glory.[48]

PRAY

     Saviour and Friend, how wonderful art Thou!
     My companion upon the changeful way,
     The comforter of its weariness,
     My guide to the Eternal Town,
     The welcome at its gate.[49]

     When the tides of the mind do cease
     Let us come, Lord, to your peace.
     When the waves rage on no more,
     Let us come, Lord, to your shore.

Lighten our darkness, we beseech thee, O Lord; and by thy great mercy defend us from all perils and dangers of this night; for the love of thine only Son, our Saviour Jesus Christ. Amen.[50]

Lord, bid me come to you across the waters.

Ri Traghad	The ebb
's ri lionadh . . .	and the flow . . .
Mar a bha	as it was
Mar a tha	as it is
Mar a bhitheas	as it shall be
Gu brath	evermore
Ri traghad	the ebb
's ri lionadh	and the flow[51]

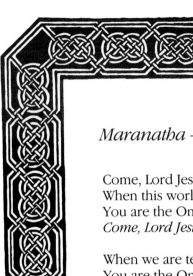

Maranatha – Come, Lord Jesus

Come, Lord Jesus.
When this world's as dark as night
You are the One we call the light.
Come, Lord Jesus.

When we are tempted to go astray
You are the One we call the way.
Come, Lord Jesus.

When we are falling in the strife
You are the One who is the life.
Come, Lord Jesus.

When troubles to our lives bring harm
You are the One who brings us calm.
Come, Lord Jesus.

When the storms of life increase
You are the One who is our peace.
Come, Lord Jesus.

When our lives are full of woe
You are the One to whom we go.
Come, Lord Jesus.

When we are down and all forlorn
Come as the resurrection morn.
Come, Lord Jesus.

When our lives are full of sin
You are the One who death does win.
Come, Lord Jesus.

Caim

The Holy Three
Protecting be
Enfolding me
In eternity
To shield
To save
To circle
To surround
My house
My home
My work
My play
Each night
Each day
Each dark
Each bright
In your light
Forever
May it be
Now
And in eternity.

Notes

———

BEGINNING – BETWEEN EBB AND FLOW

1   Gerard Manley Hopkins, 'Heaven-Haven'.
2   Arthur Hugh Clough, 'Say Not the Struggle Naught Availeth'.
3   *Tides and Seasons.*
4   H. J. Massingham, *The Tree of Life*, Chapman and Hall 1943.
5   Gerard Manley Hopkins, 'God's Grandeur'.

BETWEEN DARKNESS AND LIGHT

1   T. S. Eliot, *Burnt Norton, Four Quartets*, Faber 1959.
2   Pierre Teilhard de Chardin, *Hymn of the Universe*, Fontana 1969.
3   Minnie Louise Hoskins, 'God Knows'.
4   I Samuel 3.1–10.
5   Alexander Carmichael, ed., *Carmina Gadelica*, Academic Press, vol. i, p. 39.
6   Athanasian Creed, *Book of Common Prayer*.
7   John 9.25.
8   Teilhard de Chardin, *Hymn of the Universe*, Collins/Fontana 1970, p. 79.
9   Teilhard de Chardin, *Le Milieu Divin*, Collins/Fontana 1964, p. 46.
10 Proverbs 20.18.
11 William Blake, 'A Memorable Fancy'.
12 John 20.11–21.24.
13 John 1.14.
14 G. R. D. McLean, *Poems of the Western Highlanders*, SPCK 1961, p. 261. Also in McLean, *Praying with Highland Christians*, SPCK/Triangle 1988, p. 30.
15 John 1.14 King James Version.
16 Matthew 25.40 Good News Bible.
17 Quoted in Victor Gollancz, *A Year of Grace*, Gollancz 1950.
18 G. S. Walker, ed., *Sancti Columbani Opera*, in series *Scriptores Latini Hiberniae* Vol. 2, Dublin Institute for Advanced Studies, 1959.
19 Julian of Norwich, *Revelations of Divine Love.*
20 *Poems of the Western Highlanders*, p. 75.

1   Robert Louis Stevenson, 'Happy Thought'.
2   T. S. Eliot, 'Choruses from *The Rock* from *Collected Poems 1909–1962*, Faber 1963.
3   See Matthew 12.43–5.
4   Psalm 84.2, *Book of Common Prayer*.
5   Alistair Maclean, *Hebridean Altars*, Edinburgh 1937, p. 77.
6   *Poems of the Western Highlanders*, p. 8; *Praying with Highland Christians*, p. 5.
7   ibid., p. 90.
8   *Carmina Gadelica*, vol. iii, p. 25.
9   Peter Toon, *Meditating upon God's Word*, Darton, Longman and Todd 1988, p. 95.
10 *Carmina Gadelica*, vol. iii, p. 339.
11 *Hebridean Altars*, p. 129.
12 *Poems of the Western Highlanders*, p. 368.
13 *Hebridean Altars*, p. 55.
14 Alternative Service Book 1980, Order for Holy Communion, p. 119.
15 *Julius Caesar*, Act iv, scene ii.
16 Ignatius Loyola, *Spiritual Exercises* (trs. Thomas Corbishley, SJ), Anthony Clarke, 1979.
17 Percy Bysshe Shelley, 'Ozymandias'.
18 T. S. Eliot, *East Coker*, V, from *Four Quartets*, Faber 1942.
19 Tacitus, *Agricola*, 30.
20 Deuteronomy 8.2–6, Jerusalem Bible.
21 Mark 1.12–13, Jerusalem Bible.
22 Isaiah 35.1–8, GNB.
23 Bede, *A History of the English Church and People*, bk.iii, ch. 23 and bk.iv. ch. 28; trs. Leo Sherley-Price, Penguin 1955, pp. 177, 256.
24 R. Campbell, *Letters from a Stoic*, Penguin 1969, p. 75.
25 Quoted in Helen Waddell, *The Desert Fathers*, Constable p. 7.
26 Thomas Merton, *The Wisdom of the Desert*, Darley Andersen Books 1988, p. 22.
27 Hosea 2.14, GNB.
28 G. R. D. McLean, 'Pilgrimage', *Poems of the Western Highlanders*, p. 55.
29 Psalm 42.1–2 *Book of Common Prayer*.
30 Maria Boulding, *The Coming of God*, SPCK 1982, p. 7.
31 Matthew 28.20 GNB.
32 Kuno Meyer, *Selections from Ancient Irish Poetry*, 1928.
33 St Augustine, *Confessions*, x.27.
34 Mark 10.46–7 GNB.
35 Psalm 139.7–10 GNB.

36 Psalm 4.9 *Book of Common Prayer.*
37 *Poems of the Western Highlanders*, p. 415.
38 St Augustine.
39 Alexander Carmichael, ed., *Carmina Gadelica*, Vol. iii, p. 29.
40 Robin Flower, *Irish Tradition*, Clarendon Press 1947, p. 42.
41 *Poems of the Western Highlanders*, p. 59; *Praying with Highland Christians*, p. 28.
42 Traditional Gaelic prayer, translated by G. R. D. McLean and quoted in Martin Reith, *God in our Midst*, SPCK 1975, p. 33.

BETWEEN WEAKNESS AND STRENGTH

1 *Hamlet*, Act ii, scene ii.
2 Quoted in Ruth Etchells, *Unafraid to Be*, IVP 1969.
3 *Hebridean Altars*, p. 95.
4 ibid., p. 60.
5 T. S. Eliot, *The Elder Statesman*, Faber 1959.
6 John 3.16.
7 Romans 8.31, 38–9 GNB.
8 Matthew 11.28 GNB.
9 2 Corinthians 4.7–9 GNB.
10 David Gascoyne, 'Fragments towards a *religio poetae*', *Collected Poems*, Oxford University Press 1965.
11 *Hebridean Altars*, p. 99.
12 Romans 8.22.
13 Psalm 24.1, *Book of Common Prayer.*
14 Alex King, *Wordsworth and the Artist's Vision*, 1966, p. 20.
15 Romans 8.28.
16 Pierre Teilhard de Chardin, *Hymn of the Universe*, p. 25.
17 Exodus 33.17 KJV.
18 Isaiah 45.3 KJV.
19 Matthew 10.29–31 GNB.
20 John 1.10–13 KJV and GNB.
21 *Hebridean Altars*, p. 99.
22 ibid., p. 92.
23 Julian of Norwich, *A Shewing of God's Love*, ed. Anna Maria Reynolds, Sheed and Ward 1984.
24 E. Milner-White, *My God, My Glory*, SPCK 1959, p. 102.
25 *Hebridean Altars*, p. 152.

BETWEEN DYING AND LIVING

1 Ann Savage, trs., *The Anglo-Saxon Chronicle*, Macmillan 1984.
2 *Principles,* Society of Sacred Mission Press, 1930.
3 G. R. D. McLean, *Poems of the Western Highlanders*, pp. 90, 89 and 87.

241

4 Psalm 23.4 KJV.
5 Isaiah 46.4 KJV.
6 John Henry Newman.
7 Charles Causley, 'I am the great sun (from a Normandy crucifix of 1632)'. *Collected Poems 1951–75*, Macmillan, 1975, p. 69.
8 John 10.10.
9 Gerard Manley Hopkins, 'The Wreck of the *Deutschland*'.
10 Luke 15.5–6 RSV.
11 Ephesians 4.9–10 KJV.
12 Oscar Wilde, *E Tenebris*.
13 Julian of Norwich, *A Shewing of God's Love*.
14 Gerard Manley Hopkins, 'The Wreck of the *Deutschland*'.
15 Isaiah 43.1–2 KJV.
16 Exodus 33.14.
17 *Poems of the Western Highlanders*, p. 333; *Praying With Highland Christians*, p. 37.
18 ibid., p. 336; *Praying With Highland Christians*, p. 36.
19 Christina Rossetti. *Selected Poems*, Carcanet 1984, p. 64.
20 Collect for the Fourth Sunday after Epiphany, *Book of Common Prayer*.
21 Luke 1.78–9.
22 Tom Stoppard, *Jumpers*, Faber 1986.
23 Gerard Manley Hopkins, *God's Grandeur*.
24 Pierre Teilhard de Chardin, *Hymn of the Universe*, p. 35.
25 *Hebridean Altars*, p. 55.
26 ibid., p. 25.
27 Philippians 4.4–8 RSV.
28 John 16.33 RSV.
29 1 Corinthians 15.57–8 RSV.
30 William Walsham How, 'For all the saints'.
31 J. Patterson Smyth, *A People's Life of Christ*, Hodder and Stoughton, p. 25.
32 2 Corinthians 4.7–9 GNB.
33 The Venerable Bede.
34 *Poems of the Western Highlanders*, p. 81.
35 From a prayer card of the Additional Curates' Society.
36 *The Oxford Book of Carols*, Oxford University Press 1928, no. 149.
37 Luke 24.5–6 GNB.
38 *Poems of the Western Highlanders*, p. 275.
39 ibid., p. 107.
40 ibid., p. 339.
41 ibid., p. 234.
42 ibid., p. 10.
43 ibid., p. 103.

44 ibid., p. 415.
45 John 21.4.
46 Kevin Crossley-Holland, *The Anglo-Saxon World*, Oxford University Press 1900, p. 53.
47 *Hebridean Altars*, p. 131.
48 ibid., p. 55.
49 ibid., p. 47.
50 *The Book of Common Prayer,* Collect for Evening Prayer.
51 Fiona MacLeod, *The Winged Destiny*, William Heinemann Ltd. 1927, p. 103.

The author and publishers would like to thank the following artists for their line drawings: Jean Freer, Denise Adam, Laura Dingle, Peter Dingle, Anne Gilbert, Jenny Pearson and Elizabeth Randles.